Career Launcher

Education

Career Launcher series

Career Launcher

Education

Ken Mondschein

Ferguson Publishing
An imprint of Infobase Publishing

Career Launcher: **Education**

Copyright © 2011 by Infobase Publishing, Inc.

Ferguson
An imprint of Infobase Publishing
132 West 31st Street
New York NY 10001

Library of Congress Cataloging-in-Publication Data

Mondschein, Ken.
    Education / Ken Mondschein.
        p. cm. — (Career launcher)
    Includes bibliographical references and index.
    ISBN-13: 978-0-8160-7963-6 (hardcover : alk. paper)
    ISBN-10: 0-8160-7963-3 (hardcover : alk. paper)
1. Education—Vocational guidance—United States.
2. Teaching—Vocational guidance—United States. I. Title.
    LB2831.58M66 2009
    370.23'73—dc22

                                                    2010011889

LB 2831.58 .M66 2009

Ferguson books are available at special discounts when purchased in bulk quantities for businesses, associations, institutions, or sales promotions. Please call our Special Sales Department in New York at (212) 967-8800 or (800) 322-8755.

You can find Ferguson on the World Wide Web at http://www.fergpubco.com

Produced by Print Matters, Inc.
Text design by A Good Thing, Inc.
Cover design by Takeshi Takahashi
Cover printed by Art Print Company, Taylor, PA
Book printed and bound by Maple Press, York, PA
Date printed: November 2010

Printed in the United States of America

10 9 8 7 6 5 4 3 2 1

This book is printed on acid-free paper.

Contents

Foreword

Education is more than one of the fastest-growing fields in the American economy: It is also one that is essential to our future. Primary, secondary, and post-secondary teachers, as well as those who provide adult education and career training, are the ones who shape the workers and citizens of tomorrow. With our economy becoming increasingly knowledge-based, ignorance is one luxury we cannot afford. What's more, the educational field provides employment to millions of men and women. However, it is also an investment whose portfolio is continually being reassessed: Education consumes billions of dollars of public funds, but its dividends are sometimes not tangible for years, or even easily measurable by the standards of our results-oriented society. With stakes like these, it is no wonder that debates surrounding this field are a perennial hot-button political issue.

The end result of these pressures is that the educational industry is undergoing a time of rapid change. Growing standardization and federal mandates are transforming how we teach and learn. Today, what it means to be a good student depends more on quantitative test results than qualitative evaluations than it ever did in the past. Legal decisions also affect access to education and give districts, administrators, and teachers new mandates. At the same time, as our nation's population becomes more diverse, so, too, do our classrooms—and education professionals must both accommodate and be sensitive to these differences even as they try to guide students toward educational success.

Just as the ways in which students are evaluated are changing, so, too, are the ways in which we rate the work that teachers do. New management techniques, drawn from the business world, make the educational industry very different from what it once was. High-stakes testing means that the success or failure of an individual, a school, and a district is focused, laser-like, on one single annual educational event. In the case of the individual student what is at stake is promotion or graduation; in the case of the teacher, it is his or her job or salary; in the case of the organization, it is funding. This means that we must, in turn, adapt our teaching styles to what will get the job done—while never losing sight of the well-being and personal development of our students. While the pressure on teachers is to devote the entirety of a semester or more to "teaching to the test," the fact is that every one of our actions will shape a whole individual.

The ways in which schools are organized are also changing. New educational philosophies have given rise to a host of alternative schools, as well as ever-changing experiments in the public sector. The charter school movement has challenged traditional district organization and funding. There are even experiments with for-profit teaching models. These changes are challenges to the familiar public school system, but they also open up new employment possibilities for teachers and administrators alike. The successful education professional of the future will be able to readily adapt to these changes without losing focus on what is most important: nurturing learning.

Higher education is changing, as well. Not only is the job market more competitive than ever, but also the number of full-time positions is shrinking. Faced with declining endowments but booming enrollments, schools rely heavily on adjunct and part-time faculty. Students are also increasingly looking for practical, business or trade-oriented majors, rather than classical liberal educations. The person who wishes to work in higher education must take account of the labor market, and carefully weigh his or her options. Is graduate school worth the uncertain payoff? Will I be able to make a long-term career in higher education?

Finally, technology is transforming the entire educational industry. This is both an opportunity and a challenge. Teachers must increasingly incorporate new technologies in the classroom, and educational standards increasingly mandate that students must be familiar with new developments. This means that many teachers must be retrained in new ways of doing things. Furthermore, new fields such as online teaching, which would have been unthinkable even a generation ago, have opened up. Also, technology has blurred the lines between private and professional life. The education professional must be prepared to seize such opportunities as they are presented, as well as meet challenges and avoid pitfalls. Doing so will require one to straddle the fence between traditional ways of teaching and new progressive approaches for the foreseeable future.

All of these things mean what happens "in the field" is quite different from the way the education professional was trained and practiced a generation ago. With a complex and ever-changing professional environment such as the one presented by modern education, a comprehensive source is good to have. *Career Launcher: Education* provides the up-and-coming education professional with the information one needs to make his or her way in this career, from the history of the educational industry to the latest statistics to the various positions and surprising career paths that one can follow. The terms and trends you need to be aware of are all covered in detail. Interviews with seasoned professionals round out the volume, making this a repository not just of data, but of experience as well.

On a personal level, I have had the distinct privilege of working in numerous capacities in education over the past 20 years. Starting out as a guidance counselor and special needs teacher in public schools, my career has gradually encompassed stints as a secondary dean of students, elementary principal, director of special education, and superintendent of schools. Concurrently, I was afforded several opportunities to teach graduate education and psychology courses to aspiring practitioners, which resulted in my assuming administrative roles in education, educational leadership and psychology graduate programs. Along the way I was influenced and guided by many highly capable, competent, and enthusiastic teachers and professors who made a personal investment in me and supported my aspirations. And as if this were not enough exposure to the world of education, I have been married to a high school mathematics teacher and department chair for nearly two decades. She has astutely questioned the value of several fads and trends in education over the years, consistently underscoring the importance of keeping schooling separate from the handmaiden of politics and focused instead on what really matters: the students.

What advice do I have for those starting out in education? While it is no substitute for an experienced mentor, heed the advice in this book. It contains most of what you need to know, and a great deal that you *ought* to know. The history, traditions, methods, and collective experience of the educational industry are of no small importance. Even as we keep our eyes on the distant horizon, we must at the same time keep track of where we came from.

Education is a noble calling. It is we, the teachers, who are truly the torchbearers of society. Children may be the future, but the task of preparing them for their future lies with us. It is our hope that this book will guide you in preparing your own future.

—Nicholas D. Young, PhD, EdD
AMERICAN INTERNATIONAL COLLEGE

Acknowledgments

Great debts are owed the following people: My mother, grandmother, and grandfather—being raised by teachers certainly the best education one could have. Richard Rothschild and David Andrews of Print Matters, for giving me the opportunity to write this book. My doctoral mentor, Richard Gyug, for being a great teacher. Finally, Nicholas Young, Vickie Hess, and Thomas Maulucci of American International College.

Introduction

"Education is a social process. Education is growth. Education is, not a preparation for life; education is life itself." These are the words of John Dewey, the great American education reformer who lived and worked in the early part of the 20th century. His statement is as true today as it was almost a hundred years ago. But what did he mean by education being not just a "social process" or "growth," but "life itself"?

In place of teeth and claws or the ability to run away from danger quickly, human beings differ from other animals in that we have been gifted with a wonderfully complex brain. Rather than relying on instinct alone, we are born natural knowledge-sponges and continue learning new skills and ideas all our lives. To survive, we have developed an intricate and complicated society that has helped to make us the dominant species on our planet. However, in order to make this society function, we must get along with one another, learn specialized tasks and jobs, and cooperate in future planning. In this sense, education is not only key to individual success, but essential to our species' survival.

But humans are more than just workers: We also communicate with one another by cultural production, creating everything from novels to dances. No one can call oneself truly educated without being familiar with these cultural products. This is also part of what Dewey meant in his statement: Education is also acculturation. It is the glue that binds human beings together. Thus, no matter whether we live in the Amazon rain forest or in the concrete jungles of Manhattan, in order to make use of our natural world and to navigate our way through society, we must learn many things and put them to good use.

Another part of what Dewey meant is that we all have a share in the great work of education. We are, each of us, a teacher. Think of the hundreds of small ways you teach other people lessons every day—whether we are reinforcing the idea of politeness by holding the door for a mother with young children or teaching a senior citizen how to send pictures via e-mail. However, education as a profession and as an industry requires special skills. Giving an informal lesson on how to use a computer is one thing; being able to hold the attention of a roomful of eight-year-olds for a whole school year in order to prepare them for a state test is quite another. The same goes for a lecture hall of 18-year-olds who would rather be playing Frisbee with their friends than listening to a biology lecture.

We call the science of teaching pedagogy, literally "speaking to the young." Of course, not all teaching is done to young people. There are countless adult- and continuing-education programs, graduate and vocational schools, and nontraditional learning centers throughout the United States and Canada. Add to this corporate training, museums and foundations, and other forms of learning, and you begin to realize the scope of the educational industry.

The task of preparing the young and old with the skills they will need in their lives and careers, and which make civilized life possible, is one of society's oldest and most honored careers. This book is intended to show would-be pedagogues, and the people such as administrators and those who perform other critical jobs in the education industry, how to get a start in their intended fields.

We will begin our study with the history of the modern educational field, the focus of Chapter 1. Education used to be very different from what it is today. Most people were farmers. The literacy rate in the Middle Ages was very low. Children learned what they needed to know from copying their elders, from working alongside adults as apprentices, and, for religious and theological subjects, from church. Books were expensive and rare, and sermons were both public entertainment and public education. Any formal education in reading, writing, and mathematics was usually also through the Church. Children living in towns might have access to private grammar schools, and the children of the rich might have private tutors.

All of this changed thanks to the invention of the movable-type printing press in the fifteenth century. With books becoming more available, literacy also increased. What is more, people began to read the Bible and think about religious matters for themselves. This helped spark the Protestant Reformation of the 16th century, in which religious thinkers such as Martin Luther thought education was important. The Puritans, who were Protestants seeking religious freedom, established public schools in Massachusetts and made education compulsory. Though education in the colonies and the early United States was unorganized, it was nonetheless effective: The 1840 census found near-universal literacy.

The big changes came in the twentieth century. To begin with, emphasis on rote memorization and physical punishment for wrong answers was changed to a more forgiving, modern model. Three events further changed American education in the twentieth century: The "high school" movement made education in the liberal arts for both young men and women common; the Great Depression led to the high school diploma becoming the ticket into the middle class; and after World War II, the GI Bill made higher education much more available.

Chapter 2, "The State of the Industry," addresses where American education is today. This is a time of great change. Our democratic society has long subscribed to the notion of "education for all," and the high-tech, service-based economy of the twenty-first century has made education more valuable than ever. A college degree, rather than a high school diploma, is now seen as mandatory for a middle-class lifestyle. Education is also becoming more centralized, with programs such as No Child Left Behind requiring "high-stakes" testing. This has led to an irresolvable conflict: Not every child is equipped to pass these tests, but the pressure is on teachers and administrators. This is especially evident in less-wealthy areas, where the education gap helps to reinforce a culture of poverty.

The class issue in American education plays out in other ways, as well. The pay in many public schools, especially in the cities, is very low. It is becoming harder and harder to attract qualified candidates to fill positions, especially in math and science, and those who do take the jobs often leave after a short time. While wealthy suburbs often have no problem attracting teachers to highly paid jobs, public schools in poorer areas cannot compete. As a result, America is falling further and further behind her international competitors. President Obama has made changing this situation one of the top priorities of his administration.

Higher education is changing, too, becoming more of a business and less of an "ivory tower." To begin with, colleges' missions are changing. Modern college students expect to be treated like consumers, exchanging money for credentials. Meanwhile, the tenure system, which has historically given college professors job security, has been replaced by underpaid part-time professors teaching more students than they can handle in order to make a living wage. Meanwhile, new PhDs are having difficulty finding full-time jobs.

We discuss not only these issues, but also wages, employment statistics and prospects, and who the up-and-coming players are— in short, all the information you need to guide your future. We also detail how emerging technology is changing education, what sort of conferences and industry events you need to know about, and how new trends get started. How to receive state certification is simple enough, but are you familiar with the textbook requisition process? What about the role of teacher-training powerhouses like the Bank School of Education in determining curriculum and methods?

Chapter 3, "On the Job," will give you the practical information you need to get ahead in the education field. Whether your goal is private or public, primary school or postgraduate, classroom or administrative, we will give you the facts you need. We list all the possible jobs and positions in each sector of the education industry, describe them, and give you an idea of your possible prospects and wages. We also show how each position fits into the big picture of the industry.

Chapter 4, "Tips for Success," is your guide to making it in the world of education. Like all professions, education has its own standards and codes of conduct—as well as an increasing number of laws and regulations. Simply finding out everything you need for accreditation in your field can sometimes seem like a minefield. Then there are the unwritten things: What is professional behavior? What should you wear? How can you find opportunities, and what should you not say on interviews? What are the possibilities for promotion? We make things easy by taking you through everything you need to know in order to get started on your chosen career path.

In the same spirit, we give you Chapter 5, "Talk Like a Pro." Here, we explain industry-specific terminology, phrases, concepts, and language that you will need to know in order to succeed. What is a paraprofessional? What is an adjunct? What is a continuing education credit, and how do you get one? "Talk Like a Pro" takes the form of an alphabetical glossary of all the essential jargon you will need to know in this business.

Related to this is the final chapter, "Resources." This includes listings of Web sites intended for both local and national audiences and other online resources. In particular, our rundown of state education standards will be useful for public school teachers. Important books and the leading national training centers will be listed and described as well. As inspiration, we also list biographies and memoirs of leading figures in the education field.

The boxed features found throughout the book also are intended to help you find your way. They include "Best Practices," which are capsule descriptions of key practices and techniques in the education field that will help you optimize your performance as an education professional; "Everyone Knows," pieces of essential information that everyone working in education should be aware of, along with suggestions for further research; "Fast Facts," brief, useful facts about the education industry such as information and statistics you can use to make yourself seem like an in-the-know professional; "Keeping In Touch," which highlight both networking skills and professional etiquette protocol by giving tips for effective business communication via e-mail, phone, and in person; "On the Cutting Edge," which describe industry standards in technology, such as smart classrooms, as well as profile emerging trends like online learning; "Problem-Solving," which articulate, in a case-study style, common problems in the education field and possible crises and their resolutions; and "Professional Ethics," case studies in ethical dilemmas and their successful resolution.

Also throughout the book, you will find interviews with professionals in the various sectors of the education field. They include educators in all sectors of the industry, from public education to museum education to coaches. Heed their words. Their many years of experience will guide you. Whether it is choosing the type of teaching that you want to go into or deciding which fork to take on a branching career path. As always, the wisdom of those who have gone before is the best guide.

Educating young minds and forming tomorrow's thinkers and doers is a rewarding job, and intellectual pleasure, and an important duty. We hope that *Career Launcher: Education* will start you down your path to not only a fulfilling career, but also personal happiness and satisfaction. Our aim is to bring you not only the things you need to know to get started, but to thrive and succeed in this challenging and rewarding field. The tools you need are in your hand. All that remains is to take the first step down the road. Remember John Dewey's words: "To find out what one is fitted to do, and to secure an opportunity to do it, is the key to happiness."

Chapter 1

Industry History

As anyone who has ever had a dog or cat knows, even animals are capable of learning. Some can be quite clever: Researchers found that when a Japanese macaque (a type of monkey) named Imo learned to wash sand off sweet potatoes by dipping them in the ocean, the members of first her family and then her tribe soon followed. Imo also learned to separate wheat from sand by tossing handfuls of the mixture into the ocean. However, only human beings have developed a wide range of mental and physical skills, and only humans have a society that gives different specialized jobs to different people, and so only humans have developed a teaching profession.

The First Pedagogical Traditions

Certainly, the teaching profession is as old as civilization itself. The ancient Egyptians and Mesopotamians had schools for scribes where boys were taught to write and keep accounts. (Formal education in the pre-modern world was seen as something for young men; we will examine how education came to be seen as important for young women later on.) The Papyrus Lansing from the twentieth dynasty of ancient Egypt (about the twelfth century B.C.E.), couched as advice to a young man, explains how much better it is to be a scribe than to do back-breaking physical labor: "Apply yourself to this noble profession...Befriend the scroll, the palette. It pleases more than wine. Writing for him who knows it is better than all other professions...It is worth more than an inheritance in Egypt, than a tomb in the west."

However, the Western pedagogical tradition is usually said to have begun in ancient Greece. The Greek system of education was called *paideia*. Through it, upper-class boys were molded into men of good character who would be responsible citizens and could be entrusted with the political leadership of the city-state. Education was clearly important to the Greeks, and there was no shortage of practitioners of *paideia*. The *sophists*, or "lovers of wisdom," of late fifth century B.C.E. Athens were professional teachers in the modern sense. For a fee, they could teach you (or your child) to find the answer to any question, govern a city-state, or develop an excellent character. In particular, they specialized in rhetoric, the art of public speaking and winning court cases—very important skills for ancient Greek public life.

In comparison to the Sophists, the famous philosopher Socrates did not charge any fees and did not care about politics or the law courts. Instead, he asked questions for the sole purpose of developing a good character in his students: What is justice? What is virtue? What is wisdom? How can we do the right thing? He is held to have said: "Whom do I call educated? First, those who manage well the circumstances they encounter day by day. Next, those who are decent and honorable in their intercourse with all men...those who hold their pleasures always under control and are not ultimately overcome by their misfortunes...those who are not spoiled by their successes, who do not desert their true selves but hold their ground steadfastly as wise and sober-minded men."

Socrates' teaching took the form of dialogues or debates. Very often, the person he was asking questions is revealed to have self-contradictory opinions or not know very much at all about the thing they professed to be expert in. Other times, he would lead the pupil toward the truth by analogous reasoning. "I am disposed to ask: 'Does teaching consist in putting questions?' Indeed, the secret of your system has just this instant dawned upon me. I seem to see the principle in which you put your questions. You lead me through the field of my own knowledge, and then by pointing out analogies to what I know, persuade me that I really know some things which hitherto, as I believed, I had no knowledge of," says a character in Xenophon's *The Economist*, one of the ancient accounts of Socrates' teaching. (Socrates himself left no writings.) Socrates' ideas and method of teaching, called the *Socratic method*, came to be widely influential.

Best Practice

Marva Collins and the Socratic Method

From 1975 to 2008, Marva Collins ran Westside Preparatory School in Garfield Park, a neighborhood of Chicago, Illinois. The students in Garfield Park were not the usual prep school students: They often came from broken homes and were raised in poverty. Many had behavioral issues and were labeled by the public school system as "learning disabled." They were, in other words, the students that no one else wanted to teach.

Marva Collins was able to reach these students using a form of Socratic method. First, she would select reading material with abstract ideas, so as to enable discussion. Then she would make sure students understood the vocabulary and could pronounce it. Then the material would be read aloud, with the whole class participating. The teacher would ask questions about the material, encouraging reasoning and abstract thought. Using her method, Marva Collins was able to turn underprivileged, neglected children who "the system" had given up on into star pupils—at less than half the cost of the Chicago public schools. As she wrote, "I have discovered few learning disabled students in my three decades of teaching. I have, however, discovered many, many victims of teaching inabilities."

Besides being influenced by the Greek model of education, the ancient Romans kept schools similar to the ones we know today. The Romans had primary schools for educating their sons in grammar, rhetoric, and the other arts. Tuition was not free, though, and the teachers could be very harsh—a boy who did not learn his lessons could be beaten. Better-off fathers, or those who wanted their sons to have more than a grammar-school education, might hire tutors or even purchase educated slaves. If a poor student in a grammar school did not learn his lessons, he might be whipped, while if a rich student did not learn his lessons, his slave might be whipped! Like the Greeks, the Romans also thought public speaking was a very important skill, and many high-ranking men were trained in rhetoric and law. (Girls and young women were not supposed to play a part in public life, but some well-off women were privately educated by tutors.)

The Romans were also important for transmitting the wisdom of the ancients to the Middle Ages. Martianus Capella, who lived in the fifth century C.E., during the decline of the empire, set down the seven liberal arts—the *trivium* of grammar, logic, and rhetoric and the *quadrivium* of arithmetic, astronomy, music, and geometry. These seven disciplines encapsulated the knowledge of the ancient world. The *trivium* allowed one to read and write in Latin, which would remain the language of the educated until modern times, as well as to share one's ideas and speak publicly—the main means of communication before print. The *quadrivium* was useful not just for keeping accounts, but an integral part of religion. Astronomy helped to determine the date and time (useful for keeping holidays), music was part of divine service, and geometry could be applied to measure land or build churches.

Judaism, meanwhile, had its own means of teaching. The Jews are known as "the People of the Book," and literacy, in order to be able to read the Torah—the Hebrew Five Books of Moses—has been very important throughout Jewish history. The Jewish community has also thought it very important to establish centers of learning in order to comment on and interpret the divine law, since after the destruction of the Temple in Jerusalem in 70 C.E., these schools and the scholars they produced became the leaders in the Jewish religion and culture. Other skills, such as medicine and law, were also often taught in these schools. As a result, wherever the Jews settled, they were often the most-educated people in the neighborhood and became leaders in commerce, science, and medicine. The schools also provided a focus for the Jewish community. In fact, the Yiddish word for a temple, *shul*, comes from the German word for "school." The descendents of these Jewish academies, known as *yeshivahs*, can be found today wherever there is a Jewish community.

Education was also important to the Islamic world. The Qur'an is believed to be the received word of Allah given to the Prophet Mohammad by the angel Gabriel in Arabic, and reading this text is the responsibility of every Muslim. Arabic thus became the common language for the Muslim world, and, as for the Jewish people, schools became important foci for the Muslim religion. The Quar'an requires Muslims to pray at specific times and facing the Qibla, which points in the direction of Mecca. Muslim scientists inherited and further developed sophisticated mathematics, such as trigonometry and algebra, in order to fulfill these obligations. Likewise, Muslim schools became centers of learning in science, medicine, and law. Today, these schools, or *madrassas*, remain important centers.

In the European Middle Ages, religion was also important to education. The Catholic Church was the main repository of the learning of the ancient world. Monks kept the trivium and quadrivium alive, and tediously recopied the literature and scientific treatises of the ancient world and the religious writings of the Church Fathers. Universities grew out of cathedral schools, at first educating priests in the proper Church rites and teaching theologians to solve questions of faith and Church law, but soon branching out as teachers began to sell their store of knowledge in response to popular demand. Merchants and townsmen began to send their children to grammar schools, and rulers began to see the usefulness of rhetoric, astronomy, and arithmetic in administrating their realms. Of course, most people did not go to school at all: Peasant children would work alongside their parents, while in towns, children might be apprenticed to a craftsman (or craftswomen) and taught a trade. However, this did not mean they were uneducated. The Church can be seen as a giant educational mission, geared toward bringing a message of salvation and proper doctrine and religious observance to all people—a message that, not coincidentally, reinforced the feudal hierarchy.

All of this began to change in the fifteenth century, when Johannes Gutenberg developed the first practical movable-type printing press. Suddenly, books were much less expensive than they had been when copied by professional scribes. People were very religious in the Middle Ages, and so not surprisingly, the Bible and religious tracts were amongst the first things printed. The literacy rate also increased dramatically, as did the number of people writing in everyday languages such as English, French, and German, rather than the scholarly Latin. However, this opened up a whole new can of worms. People could now not only read about religion for themselves, but they could also express their ideas and distribute them for a relatively low cost. In many ways, the fifteenth century was the first Information Age.

The result of all this education, combined with the state of European politics at the time, was nothing short of a revolution. In 1517, a German priest named Martin Luther nailed his famous 95 Theses to the door of the church in Wittenberg, objecting to the Church's sale of indulgences, that is, the forgiving of sins for money. The Church soon declared him a rebel and a heretic. Unlike earlier people with such ideas, who had been able to be suppressed, Luther had the printing press at his disposal. Soon, people all over Germany were discussing his ideas—in German, not Latin. The Bible was also translated and printed in German. The result was a widespread religious and political movement that we today call the Protestant Reformation. One of the core Protestant beliefs was the importance of education, so that people could read the Bible and learn about God for themselves. To counter this, the Church (now the Roman Catholic Church) set up their own educational mission to argue their point of view. The result was a war of ideas for the hearts and minds of Europe—and the population as a whole growing more educated and sophisticated.

The Birth of Modern Education

You may have noticed that we have been talking almost exclusively about education for boys and young men. Though there were many exceptions and examples of learned women—the abbess Heloise, the French writer Christine de Pisan, the German polymath Hildegard of Bingen, the English mystic Julian of Norwich—these women were elite and therefore unusual. The idea that young women ought to be educated as well as young men, as well as the idea of the public school and indeed modern education itself, may be traced back to the Enlightenment.

What is the Enlightenment? Though this term is used in many senses, and can mean different things, generally it is considered to be the renewed faith in human reason and the ability of human beings to decide the course of their own society without slavishly following the past or looking for divine guidance. The Enlightenment in this sense was mostly a French and British phenomenon, and it mainly occurred over the course of the late seventeenth and eighteenth centuries. It is marked not only by an urge toward parliamentary, democratic systems, but also the beginnings of modern capitalism—reforms that were more successfully instituted in England in France, which, amongst other reasons, is why the French Revolution occurred at the end of the eighteenth century. Enlightenment ideas were also critical to the establishment of the new government in the United States, and are enshrined in our Constitution.

Part of Enlightenment philosophy, of course, was education. If men were to build their own utopia (and most Enlightenment philosophers firmly felt that society should be in the hands of men), then they would have to be trained for this task. New ideas of "natural" education began to take hold. For instance, in the Enlightenment philosopher Jean-Jacques Rousseau's 1762 novel *Emile*, the titular character was brought to understand reasoning and logic, select a trade, and lastly to be educated in "sentimental" virtues such as love of country and religion. Rousseau's emphasis was on remaining virtuous in a corrupt society and on forming a man into a *citizen*; he also made much of the idea that children develop in stages:

> Education comes from nature, from men or from things. The inner growth of our organs and faculties is the education of nature, the use we learn to make of our growth is the education of men, what we gain by our experience of our surroundings is the education of things. Thus we are each taught by three masters. If their teaching conflicts, the scholar is ill-educated and will never be at peace with himself; if their teaching agrees, he goes straight to his goal, he lives at peace with himself, he is well-educated.

Fast Facts

Jesuit Education Principles

One of the Roman Catholic Church's weapons in fighting the Protestant Reformation was the Society of Jesus, or Jesuits, founded in 1534 by a former Spanish soldier named Ignatius Loyola. Loyola saw his new order's main missions as educating worthy young people without regard to their wealth or family position. To do so, he formulated a set of educational principles. One of these was *cura personalis*, literally "care of the person," but perhaps better translated as "individual attention." What this means is, firstly, that the whole person must be educated: intellectually, physically, spiritually, and morally. In many ways, this draws from the classical model proposed by the ancient Greeks and continued by the Romans.

Cura personalis also means that each student is different and responds differently to challenges and will grow in their own way. They come from different backgrounds, and have unique gifts and insights. Therefore, rather than trying to fit all students into a mold, a teacher should pay attention to each pupil as an individual. It is also interpreted today to mean that each individual is worthy and deserving of being educated.

Today, Jesuits continue their educational mission. There are hundreds of Jesuit colleges and universities around the world—28 in the United States—as well as many primary and secondary schools.

Everyone

Knows

What Do Those Letters Mean?

The BA or BS on your college degree stand for "bachelor of arts" and "bachelor of science," with the former usually being awarded for degrees in languages, literature, history, and other subjects, while the latter is reserved for degrees in science and technology.

Some schools, such as Harvard, have AB and SB, which are the initials for the old Latin *artium baccalaureus* and *scientium bacca-laureus*. In the "ancient universities" of the United Kingdom and Ireland—Oxford, Cambridge, and Dublin's Trinity College—those who graduate with degrees in science are also given BA degrees. The "bachelor's" refers not to the recipient's being married or unmarried, but to the Latin. The exact origin is unclear, though it was in use as early as the thirteenth century.

In addition to these degrees, the modern system of higher education has cooked up a veritable alphabet soup:

BFA: Bachelor of fine arts, generally given to those who have graduated with a professional degree in visual or performing arts (such as from a conservatory).

BSW: Bachelor of social work.

Note that Rousseau says *men*, not *people*. Young women's education was still seen as different from, and less essential than, young men's. Emile's wife-to-be, Sophie, was only educated insofar as would enable her to be a good wife and to raise intelligent children for her husband and her society. However, the fact that Rousseau discussed women's education at all was nothing short of revolutionary. Writers such as Mary Wollstonecraft, in her *Vindication of the Rights of Woman*, would take up this banner, arguing that since men and women are equal in their reasoning ability, they ought to be educated equally in an enlightened world. If women are foolish or superficial, she wrote, it is because men have made them that way. As she wrote, "My main argument is built on this simple principle, that if she be not prepared by education to become the companion of man, she will stop the

MA: Master of arts, the first level of postgraduate study in arts after the bachelor's degree. The master's degree is so-named because it was the degree that a full professor, or *magister*, in the medieval university received. (In the Middle Ages, all you needed to teach at the university level was a bachelor's degree; today, the master's is the minimum.)

MBA: Master of business administration, for those who study scientific approaches to management of business and industry.

MFA: Master of fine arts, awarded for graduate education in the arts such as dance, writing, sculpture, etc.

MPA: Master of public administration

MS: Master of science, the MA equivalent for the sciences.

PhD: Meaning *philosophiae doctor*, or "doctor of philosophy," this degree entitles the recipient to the title "doctor." The reason is because "doctor," in Latin, means "teacher," and comes from the medieval *licentia docendi*, or license to teach. It is only comparatively recently that physicians became "doctors" instead of philosophers! The PhD is the highest level of education that can be awarded in any field, and is usually required for those seeking a career as university professors.

EdD: Doctorate in the field of education.

progress of knowledge, for truth must be common to all, or it will be inefficacious with respect to its influence on general practice."

Olympe des Gouges, a beautiful, educated, and radical Frenchwoman who had been born into a humble family but rose in the ranks of the Parisian intelligentsia, penned an eloquent defense of the rights of women during the French Revolution. Women can ascend the scaffold as condemned political criminals, she wrote; it is only proper that they ought to ascend the rostrum as political speakers. By extension, women's intellectual gifts ought to be as nourished as men's. However, Olympe des Gouges' writings on the "Rights of Women" earned her only a scaffold of her own. She was executed by guillotine by revolutionaries who thought that the public sphere should belong exclusively to men.

Still, we can see in Mary Wollstonecraft and Olympe des Gouges a radical possibility: If people of all different classes are able to be leaders in society, then why not people of both genders? It is to Enlightenment ideas about the dignity and capability for education of all people that we can attribute the movements for women's education and the education of all classes of society in the following centuries. These ideas went hand-in-hand with new concepts of democracy and civil life. In many ways, the world we are living in today is a product of Enlightenment ideas. However, faith in reason was not the only factor that influenced modern education. Religion had a part to play, as well.

Education in Early America

The British colonies and the early United States were far ahead of Europe in terms of education. Part of this was because of Enlightenment ideas about the inherent worth (and potential for education) of all people, and partly because of the colonies' origins as a haven for oppressed Protestants such as the Pilgrims, who placed great importance on reading the Bible. The Boston Latin School, the first Latin grammar school, was established in 1635, 15 years after the Pilgrims landed, to provide a classical education to the children of the elite. The first "free school" was opened in the Virginia colony in the same year. Beginning in 1642, education in the Massachusetts Bay Colony was made compulsory; other colonies soon followed. Massachusetts was also home to the first American institute of higher education, Harvard University, which opened its doors in 1638. The United States was also an early leader in education for women: One of the first schools for girls, the "Little Girls' School," was founded in 1772 by the Moravians, a Protestant group from central Europe who established the village of Salem in North Carolina; it eventually became an "academy," or high school, and became known as Salem College in 1907. (The first institute of higher education for women, Mount Holyoke Female Seminary—today Mount Holyoke College—did not open until 1837.)

Early American communities supported schools and paid for them through taxes. The Land Ordinance of 1785 set aside a portion of the land in every township in the unincorporated territories to use to support public education. As a result, by the 1840s, literacy was almost universal in the United States. About 55 percent of the 3.6 million boys and girls in the United States attended primary schools; most of the rest were educated at home. Boston English

High School, the first public high school, opened in 1821; by 1827 Massachusetts required all towns with more than 500 families to have a public high school. There were also advances made in education of the disabled: The Connecticut Asylum at Hartford for the Instruction of Deaf and Dumb Persons opened in 1817.

Education was seen as essential to the new Republic. To begin with, democracy requires an educated citizenry who are able to read newspapers and debate issues. Also, Americans were by and large Protestants, and considered it important to read the Bible. Of course, this did not extend to everyone: Most African Americans lived in slavery until the 1860s, and it was forbidden to educate them. The same forces that kept African Americans in bondage also recognized the liberating power of education. Nonetheless, many African Americans managed to obtain educations, and the writings of former slaves such as Harriet Jacobs, Frederick Douglas, and Boston King are some of the most powerful and compelling historical narratives of that time, as well as powerful cases for universal rights and the inherent dignity of all people.

The Modern Age of Education

Two powerful changes took place in nineteenth-century America. The first was the founding of "normal schools," that is, teacher-training institutes. Most teachers in the early Republic were not formally trained. Becoming a schoolteacher required no credentials, and hiring was up to the local school board. By the end of the century, the vast majority of schoolteachers had been through two years of a normal school. This had a tremendous impact on both the quality and uniformity of education.

The second major change was the establishment of public education systems. Unlike the earlier, locally based schools, these were funded through public monies and had established curriculums and standards for teachers. Educational reformers such as Horace Mann in Massachusetts advocated public education for all, which was reinforced by laws that required parents to send their children to school. The U.S. public education system was highly influenced by the educational system developed in Prussia, in modern Germany, which was admired for forging a strong central state. It was also spurred on by Reconstruction, which had a strong interest in seeing the South reintegrated into the Union. By 1870, every state in the Union had free elementary education.

Why this change in methods and philosophy? The shift took place for several reasons. First, education was also held to help immigrants assimilate. In 19th-century America, as now, there was a great deal of anxiety about "un-American" newcomers changing the makeup of the Republic. Such immigrants had foreign languages, foreign beliefs, and foreign customs. Mandatory public schooling would mold them into "Americans," teaching them English, work ethics, and Anglo-Saxon customs—by force, if necessary. This legacy remains today: Education is the fire that heats up the American melting pot. However, unlike today, the dignity of individuals and individual cultures was not a concern, only that they conform to "American" norms.

We can see from this idea that education can also be a highly effective form of propaganda. In other words, it can be used to get people to think the way you want them to—for religious, political, or social motives. Nineteenth- and early twentieth-century educational theorists were not concerned with developing the character and ability of each individual. Rather, their end goal was the second reason for the great expansion of American education: To produce the sort of industrial-age workforce that would fuel the machine of American industry. For the vast majority of people, school was a place to learn to be good—which is to say obedient—citizens, and good—that is, productive—workers for the industrial machine. As Elwood Cubberly, a prominent educator, wrote in his 1905 dissertation for Columbia Teachers College, schools should be like factories, "in which raw products, children, are to be shaped and formed into finished products... manufactured like nails, and the specifications for manufacturing will come from government and industry."

Needless to say many people considered these assumptions to be racist, xenophobic, classist, and geared toward stamping out the unique cultures they had brought with them to the New World. They wanted their children to become Americans, but still keep elements of their way of life. This urge was especially strong with Catholic immigrants from Italy, Poland, and Ireland. In response, Catholic organizations set up their own system of Catholic schools. John Joseph Hughes, Archbishop of New York, was a leader in this, protesting the mandatory use of the (Protestant) King James Bible in schools and founding a number of colleges, including the renowned Fordham University. He also saw these schools as a way to educate the young men and women of these often poverty-stricken immigrants in good habits, moral behavior, and work ethics. This was the third factor fueling the great growth in American education: For groups who felt excluded from the American dream to take a piece of it for themselves through education.

These schools were funded exclusively by the parishes themselves. Catholic parents paid taxes into the general public education fund, then also school fees to the parish. Thanks to the Blaine Amendments (named after Senator James G. Blaine of Maine, who, like many Protestant Nativists, feared the growing Catholic influence) added to most state constitutions in the 1870s, no public monies could be used to fund religious schooling. Though the 2002 Supreme Court decision *Zelman v. Simmons-Harris* partially dismantled these amendments, saying that Ohio's Pilot Project Scholarship Program could indeed pay for parents to send their children to religious as well as secular private schools, no state school system has taken advantage of this. (This is somewhat ironic, since Blaine amendments were originally instituted by Protestants to block Catholics, whereas current opposition to this legislation is headed by conservative or evangelical Protestant organizations.)

Education for African Americans was likewise an important issue in the years after the Civil War. Activists such as Booker T. Washington and W. E. B. DuBois believed that education was important for African Americans to achieve true freedom. Washington was a proponent of "self-help" and education, leading the Tuskegee Normal and Industrial Institute and tirelessly lecturing and publishing until his death from overwork in 1915. As the title of his home institution indicates, Washington favored trade-oriented education. The Harvard-educated (and unabashedly Communist) DuBois, however, thought that working as an industrial proletariat was little better than slavery, and favored organizing under the "talented tenth" of African American leadership to improve the lot of all.

The difference of opinion between Washington and DuBois echoes a broader debate in American education taking place in the late nineteenth and early twentieth centuries. Some thought, as discussed above, that it was best if a state-run education system was geared toward forming a loyal, hard-working industrial class. Others believed that it was wrong to limit human potential in this way, and that education in languages, literature, higher mathematics— the liberal arts—should be available to all. The "high school" movement, which is considered to have lasted from 1910 to 1940, saw a

INTERVIEW

"Be Ready to Do Anything"

R. J. Ferullo
Special education teacher, Northampton, Massachusetts

How long have you been a special education teacher? How did you start?
I have been a special education teacher for 12 years, working in school systems across the state. I have worked with kids with a variety of disabilities from moderate learning disabilities to students with autism. I started in special education right out of college because I pretty much needed a job, and found one as a tutor in a special ed department. From there I found I really enjoyed working with a population that really needed a little extra help to get through the school day.

What qualifications do you need?
Training required classes and a college degree. A state mandated teacher test is required for certification, as well as continuing education classes directly related to the field of special ed. After that, there are always courses to take to stay on top of information related to the field.

massive increase in this higher-level education. In the beginning of this period, less than one in five American teenagers had attended high school; by the end about three in four did.

American high school education was truly something unique. Rather than preparing the vast majority of people for the trades, as in Europe, high schools provided education "for life" and had an emphasis on social mobility, academic instruction, and access for all. Unlike the centrally planned and regulated European schools, American high schools were locally regulated. The postwar boom in the ranks of the middle class was made possible by the growth in high schools; a diploma became the entry-level requirement to a good job. Moreover, high schools changed American culture: The social focus of teenage life shifted from home, work, and the local community to the school. Because they were open to both genders, they also contributed to the massive twentieth-century increase in

What are the challenges and rewards?

Challenges relate to the multiple issues individual kids need on a daily basis, but rewards come as you see students make connections and learn things you are teaching, and things you are not expecting to teach. Working in special education, you work closer to a small number of students than a general education subject teacher. Relationships that develop are different, and since you get to know the kids, you begin to care about the kids more.

Why should someone choose special education as a career? What advice to you have for someone who might want to go into this field?

As to why some one would consider pursuing this path as a career: It really is an individual thing. I think some people want to work in special education because you do make a more direct difference in the lives of the students in the school. With that however comes a greater responsibility to the individual students that you work. As opposed to kids leaving at the end of the school day or even the school year, a special education teacher can work with the same kids for several years and the student becomes part of the teacher's life.

My best advice to someone who is just starting out is to take each day as it comes. That each student has individual differences and individual needs, and someone starting in the field should be ready to do anything to help out your students.

women's education, women's enrollment in college, women's rights, and—not coincidentally—women's employment.

Schools were also an important battleground in the battle for civil rights. The 1896 Supreme Court ruling *Plessy v. Ferguson* made segregation legal. In 1951, thirteen Topeka, Kansas, parents tried to enroll their children in a white school in the city's segregated school district. The resulting lawsuit, known as *Brown v. Board of Education*, ended in a landmark 1954 Supreme Court decision. "Separate but equal" was recognized as inherently unequal. The *de jure* integration was made *de facto* by such incidents as Little Rock Integration Crisis of 1957, in which President Eisenhower ordered elements of the regular Army into peacetime action on U.S. soil in response to Arkansas governor Oval Faubus' calling out of his state's National Guard to prevent the integration of Little Rock High School. Eisenhower also ordered federal marshals to confront Alabama governor George

Wallace and to move him from his "Stand at the Schoolhouse Door" at the University of Alabama in 1963.

One of the results of the Civil Rights Act was the unpopular "desegregation bussing" (or "forced bussing"), when it was felt that since some schools were, due to district demographic make-ups, almost all-black or all-white, students should be assigned to schools based on race. The plan was applied to northern cities, such as Boston and Detroit, as well as southern ones. However, bussing was a resounding failure: In addition to being limited by later Supreme Court decisions to only those cases where there was intentional segregation across multiple districts and being shown as ineffectual, bussing led to protests and even violence, and was also easy to circumvent, since many parents would rather move their children to the suburbs or into private schools than have them attend a school that they thought was inferior. Today, bussing is not as much of an issue: students are assigned to schools by more sophisticated computer systems and specialist magnet schools that "draw" students across district lines have increased in popularity. However, it foretold an important trend in late twentieth-century public education: Increasing central oversight and wresting schools from community and local control.

Higher Education after World War II

World War II had an important effect on both the American economy and education. Faced with a massive labor glut from returning and soon-to-be-unemployed service members and concerned with the effects this would have on the newly recovered economy, Congress passed the Servicemen's Readjustment Act of 1944, better known as the GI Bill. Besides giving veterans unemployment and mortgage benefits, one of the provisions was that the government would pay toward college or trade school tuition. By 1965, 1.2 million veterans had gone to college on the GI Bill, over 860,000 had used it for other education, and 318,000 had sought occupational training. The result was a dramatic increase in the educated, home-owning middle class. A college education was now within reach of most people.

In response to this demand for postsecondary education, a sea change occurred in American higher education. Previously, most colleges and universities had been small and privately owned. Only a very small elite attended, or indeed needed to attend, these institutions. Now, public university systems expanded enormously, with New York and California's systems leading the way. In 1930, only 122,000 college graduates were granted degrees in the whole of the United States; in 1950, the number was 432,000. Thereafter, the population of the nation's campuses increased dramatically: There were 2.5 million college students enrolled in 1955; 3.6 million in 1960; and, by 1966, over 6 million. At least some college education was the new ticket to the middle class.

Those who aspired to a better life than their parents' would be required to jump the hurdles in the paper chase toward a college diploma.

Community colleges are another important element in the higher-educational system. Once called "junior colleges," these had their origins in the late nineteenth century when academics and educators would tour the country, offering brief courses in an environment similar to religious meetings. The best example was the Chautauqua adult-education movement, named after its start as a Sunday-school teachers' program on the shores of Lake Chautauqua in New York State in 1874. The wide-flung farming and ranching communities of nineteenth- and early twentieth-century America were eager for the culture and entertainment that these meetings brought.

Other two-year schools grew out of high schools, the first being Joliet Junior College, founded in Joliet, Illinois, in 1901. The number of such schools was sufficient for the American Association of Junior Colleges to be established in the 1920s. Like the Chautauqua movement, these schools met a need for a level of education that was more accessible and less expensive than four-year universities, but greater than high school. Some were intended for graduates to transfer to four-year schools; others were normal schools dedicated to teacher training. In the era after World War II, two-year colleges, like the rest of the higher-education system, benefited from the increase of government interest and the GI Bill. The Baby Boomer generation increased enrollment tremendously. Today, "junior college" tends to refer to a private two-year postsecondary school, while community colleges are publicly supported. There are 1,166 community colleges in the United States today. Advocates point out that they are useful for educating those who would otherwise not go to college, especially in vocational fields, and giving older workers new skills. Critics charge that they keep people in the working class from pursuing excellence in education, discourage transferring, and train workers for private industry at public expense.

The increase in college education also emphasized a trend in American education and job-preparedness that would continue through the twenty-first century: A new emphasis on knowledge-work and academic subjects, with a parallel devaluing of physical labor. The new rule was that academic preparation was to be a focus for all students. Having "only" a high school diploma, once seen as the entry to the middle class, was now seen as the sign of educational failure.

Higher education also changed as a result of this new inclusiveness. College education began to shift from purely academic subjects to what can be described as "vocational" subjects. Whereas the students of yesteryear were free to study "useless" liberal arts subjects, one could now major in business or accounting with an aim toward finding practical employment in the new white-collar economy, or continuing on to a professional degree in disciplines such as law or medicine. Many have critiqued the new, practical focus, complaining that it undermines the purpose of higher education and lowers standards. Nonetheless, it remains a practical adaptation necessary for the new market and new labor conditions. It also meant that the boundaries between the elites and non-elites—admission to prestigious colleges and universities—became more important, and harder to hurdle, than ever.

The ways in which people pay for college were also affected by federal legislation. Originally, of course, college was out-of-pocket (and thus limited to the well-off) or there were select scholarships. For instance, a community or church might take up a collection to send its brightest pupil to train to be a preacher. The GI Bill, by making federal money available for higher education, vastly increased the number of people able to attend college. The Higher Education Act of 1965, part of Lyndon Johnson's "Great Society" program, went even further. For instance, it provided for Stafford Loans, loans backed by the federal government and intended for individuals to pay for their college or postgraduate educations. Another example is the Pell Grant, introduced by legislation proposed by Senator Clairborne Pell in 1965 to provide college education grants to low-income families. However, the main method of financing college for the majority of people remains both federal and private loans and their own money.

Financing higher education in the United States thus usually comes down to the individual. In this, there is a sharp contrast with Europe, where the state pays for most of the cost.

Recent History

As noted earlier, the most notable shift in American education in recent years has been a gradual change from local control to more centralized, even federal, oversight. In many ways, this is more of the European model, and it is a decidedly mixed blessing. Centralized control can lead to more funds being available for resources and lead to higher and more uniform standards. It is difficult, for instance, for a local or state school board to forbid (for instance) the teaching of evolution when federal standards mandate it, or for them to set standards that are below the national average. However, it can also lead to difficulties, especially when educational goals are set by political agendas and not children's needs, or when priorities conflict.

Special education is a positive example of increased federal control. Previously, it was very hard to find non-institutional services for those with physical or mental handicaps; many children were institutionalized needlessly, simply for lack of other resources. The movement toward education of those with disabilities had been growing since the 1950s, with Civitan clubs leading the way in providing specific teacher training. This culminated with the 1975 Education for All Handicapped Children Act, which requires school districts to provide equal access to education. The act has since provided the basis for parents fighting to get fair treatment for children with disabilities. (Unfortunately, providing funding for such programs is another matter.)

Increased federal funding has also been beneficial in many ways. Head Start is one such example. It began in 1961 under the Department of Health and Human Services, and was revised under the Head Start Act of 1981. By 2005, over 22 million children had participated. The 2005 budget also allocated $6.9 million for 905,000 children. It is aimed not only at giving low-income children healthy early childhoods, but also providing educational intervention. Though some have criticized the program, saying that any early gains tend to fade in primary school or are washed away by the environment of disadvantaged schools, others hold that children who have completed Head Start are more likely to complete school and go to college and less likely to be charged with a crime by their early 20s.

Another huge, and closely related, change is the application of business principles to teaching. Modern business, taking "if you cannot measure it, you cannot manage it" as its mantra, places a high emphasis on metrics—being able to quantify every last thing. If a child's ability to read cannot be reduced to a data point, then that child might as well not know how to read. Accordingly, a new emphasis has been placed on standardized testing. Closely related to this is the philosophy of "standards-based education." This philosophy is based on management principles, especially the emphasis on metrics and high-stakes testing. It holds that by setting high standards and measuring performance, a quantifiable improvement in education can be observed. In this, it sets itself in opposition to "norm-based" testing, where students are ranked relatively in comparison to one another. "Standards-based" education sets one objective norm that all students must reach. Standardized test scores are therefore very important to this school of thought. By setting these baselines and holding all students to the same criteria, it aims to eliminate racial, ethnic, and regional differences in education. Children growing up in single-parent families in the inner city or in poor rural communities are expected to reach the same standards as those from comfortable middle-class suburbs.

"No Child Left Behind" (NCLB, often pronounced "nickelbee"), a federal initiative proposed by President George W. Bush and passed by Congress in 2002, is a good example of how the "standards-based" approach is applied and how the federal government is, through its deep pockets, gradually exerting more and more influence on American education. The federal government spent $42.2 billion on education in 2001; in 2007, it was $54.4 billion. Of this, NCLB went from receiving $17.4 billion in 2001 to $24.4 billion in 2007.

NCLB is making itself felt in a number of ways. Firstly, it calls for every state to test every student every year. Secondly, it calls for every public school and district to display "Adequate Yearly Progress" (AYP), with the goal of 100 percent of students being proficient by the 2013–2014 school year. The various states have the freedom to implement this as they see fit. Illinois, for instance, requires that 95 percent of all students be tested in reading and mathematics and that 95 percent pass the test.

NCLB standards have thus led to a massive increase in so-called high-stakes testing—*high stakes* being a term aptly taken from gambling, since the consequences for failure are very grave. For instance, a student who does not pass a high-stakes test might not be promoted to the next grade or receive a diploma. A school or district that does not have a certain percentage of students pass a test might lose funding, and teachers might even be fired. NLCB provides specific penalties for schools that fail to make "Adequate Yearly Progress" two or more years in a row: Parents are given the option to send their children to other schools, and the school must offer tutoring after-school programs. These can be very expensive in an era of already-tight budgets.

The fact that NCLB metrics hold all students and all schools to the same standard when conditions are manifestly not the same across all schools and situations and gives severe penalties for not meeting these standards is often criticized as unfair. Some point out that talented teachers are less likely to work in at-risk situations, where they will be penalized for attempting to reach the most difficult students. Also, many complain that teachers are forced to "teach to the test," and that this is not conducive to learning abstract thinking or real problem-solving skills. It also makes academic dishonesty more likely, gives incentives to cheat, and makes students who do not test well more likely to be marginalized in special education or other testing-exempt classes. The fact that there is an incentive for making the standards low enough for all students to pass means that bright students are not challenged. It also emphasizes a narrow curriculum of math and reading—no social studies, no physical education, no literature, no science. Foreign language-speaking students are only given three years to achieve sufficient proficiency to take the test in English. Finally, many charge that merely expecting teachers to pull testing miracles out of their hats without addressing underlying socioeconomic causes of poor academic performance—teenage pregnancies, lack of child care, a culture of poverty—is unrealistic. However, as we have seen, the penalties for *not* reaching the standards are severe.

The increase in spending and in central control means that education has become big business. For instance, the state of Texas, because it begins its textbook adoption cycle before other states' and because it is a large market, has disproportionate influence on the textbook market. Many other states follow Texas' lead in deciding what curriculum to set. The State of Texas' adoption committees, in turn, tend to be beholden to special interests with specific agendas.

Prospects for Higher Education

"In a 21st century economy where the most valuable skill you can sell is your knowledge, education is the single best bet we can make—not just for our individual success, but for the success of the nation as a whole," President Barack Obama said in a speech on March 10, 2009. Indeed, the twenty-first century is looking to be an era in which knowledge—and educational credentials—are at a premium. President Obama has repeatedly stated that every American should have at least one year of postsecondary schooling. However, he was careful to not specify that this should be *academic* schooling. Job training is equally important, as are community colleges, which are critical to providing vocational training for careers such as nursing and in providing a gateway to four-year schools.

The Obama administration has also sought to recognize the fact that we live in a dynamic economy and that many adults go back to school, either to earn a postsecondary degree for the first time, to improve their credentials, or to change career paths entirely. In recognition of these facts, Pell grants have been made available to unemployed adults for the first time. Those enrolled in education or training programs are now also allowed, unlike in the past, to keep their unemployment benefits. Furthermore, earnings from lost jobs are not included in the reckoning of eligibility for such programs.

In many ways, this reflects a change from previous policy and reflects more of the real labor situation than the world that many academics envision. Not everyone wants to, or can, participate in the "knowledge economy." A cubicle and computer screen is not, and should not be, the end point of everyone's academic journey. In the past, children who did not excel in academic subjects were given options for vocational education; this is not so much the case today. As Matthew B. Crawford, a University of Chicago PhD in political philosophy-turned-motorcycle mechanic, put it in his 2009 book *Shop Class as Soulcraft*, "The imperative of the last 20 years to round up every warm body and send it to college, then to the cubicle, was tied to a vision of the future in which we somehow take leave of material reality and glide about in a pure information economy. This has not come to pass. To begin with, such work often feels more enervating than gliding. More fundamentally, now as ever, somebody has to actually do things: fix our cars, unclog our toilets, build our houses."

Part of the problem is that skilled manual labor has been held in low esteem in the postwar years. However, tasks in which a person has to be physically present to perform some sort of skilled work—fixing engines, laying power lines, installing plumbing—will always have to be done. Workers with the necessary skills and qualifications will always be in high demand, and many people prefer doing physical work where the end result can be seen and felt to the often-enervating abstract work that can be done on a computer screen. The growing realization that not everyone is academically oriented, or is happy to sit at a desk for eight to 10 hours a day, means that the skilled trades are gaining in prestige and being seen as worthwhile career paths. Accordingly, the demand for trade schools and vocational programs will only grow. For the education professional, this opens up many possibilities—and also means that many who would not think of becoming educators can.

Distance learning is another educational format that has become popular with the rise of the Internet. While correspondence courses in shorthand have been known since the eighteenth century, and the rise of regular mails made degrees in academic subjects offered by post feasible since the late nineteenth century, broadband Internet has given this field exciting new possibilities. Classes can now "meet" and professors can lecture and post course materials in real time, giving the experience more human interaction than ever before. Most colleges and universities offer at least some distance learning, and some, such as the University of Phoenix, offer a catalog composed entirely of online courses. Now, as in the past, the market for such learning remains the same: People not able to physically attend regular classes—formerly, because they lived far from centers of learning or because of the demands of work life; today, because of their over-scheduled modern lives.

The Growth in Alternative Education

As we saw above, historically most private schools have been religious. However, a growing dissatisfaction with the educational system has meant that secular alternatives to mainstream education have been cropping up. Foremost amongst these is the Montessori method, developed by Maria Montessori, an Italian educator who lived from 1870 to 1952. Billing itself as "child-centered," the Montessori method has teachers, known as "directors," not teaching in the formal sense, but rather presenting carefully chosen and constructed materials that engage all five senses and allow children to explore their world and derive concepts and abstract principles. Each child is treated as an individual and not forced into a particular mold, since the Montessori method believes that children's learning ultimately takes place in self-chosen moments of intense concentration. We will deal more with Montessori and other alternative education trends in the next chapter.

Homeschooling is another recent movement. Some homeschooling parents are certainly religiously motivated, but a 2003 U.S. Census survey revealed that only about a third cited religious grounds as their reason. The growth of the movement (over 1.1 million children in 2003, or 2.2 percent of the student population) means that homeschoolers have reached a critical mass. Homeschooling parents in the same region form co-operative ventures to pool talents and resources, and even hire outside tutors. This, in turn, offers new opportunities for education professionals. Homeschoolers also make great use of distance learning to enrich their curriculum.

Within the world of state-supported schooling, alternative schools and the magnet school movement are two significant changes in the educational landscape. A magnet school offers special programs—in science or languages, for example—in addition to the standard curriculum, drawing students from across district lines like iron filings to a magnet. An alternative school is any school that that differs from the norm, and as such is impossible to describe categorically. They may cater to students with physical, mental, or emotional difficulties; unusually bright students who engage in self-directed learning; or employ unusual pedagogical techniques. The Harvey Milk School in New York City was chartered to provide a safe and supportive school space for lesbian, gay, bisexual, transgender or questioning teenagers. The diversity offered by these mini-schools, when compared to the NCLB mandates of the public schools, can be seen as a microcosm of current trends and conflicts in education: The drive for greater centralization and conformity, set against the growing acknowledgement that children and adults have different needs than some imagined norm.

A Brief Chronology

Fortieth–twenty-sixth centuries B.C.E.: Writing develops in ancient Mesopotamia.

Fifth–fourth centuries B.C.E.: Lives of Socrates, Plato, Aristotle, and Confucius.

Third century c.e.: Jewish scholars begin to compile the Talmud.

Fifth century c.e.: Martianus Capella codifies the *trivium* and *quadrivium*.

Seventh century c.e.: Islamic schools begin to be founded.

c. 1160: The University of Paris is founded.

c. 1439: Gutenberg invents the movable-type printing press.

1517: Martin Luther begins the Protestant Reformation.

1534: The Society of Jesus (Jesuits) is founded.

1630s: The Boston Latin School and Harvard University are founded.

1642: Education is made compulsory in the Massachusetts Bay Colony.

1762: Rousseau publishes *Emile*.

1785: The U.S. Congress passes the Land Ordinance.

1837: Mount Holyoke Female Seminary (later Mount Holyoke College), the first institute of higher education for women, is founded.

1841: Fordham University founded as St. John's College.

1870: Birth of Maria Montessori.

1870s: Blaine Amendments added to U.S. state constitutions.

1944: The GI Bill is passed.

1954: *Brown v. Board of Education* is tried at the U.S. Supreme Court.

1975: Education for All Handicapped Children Act is passed.

1981: Head Start Act is passed.

2002: No Child Left Behind Act is passed.

Chapter 2

State of the Industry

The education industry in America, whether public or private, primary or postsecondary, is undergoing rapid change. Growing standardization and centralization are affecting all levels of public education and seem poised to spill into higher education, as well. On the other hand, there is also a growing movement toward privatization, non-government management, and decentralized charter schools. The intersection of these two opposing forces has led to some interesting developments, such as a turn to independently run schools in response to more traditional models not meeting federally mandated standards. Likewise, faced with short resources and increasing competition, colleges and universities as well as public school districts are being forced to rethink how they distribute their limited funds. Changes in the labor market are also affecting both sectors, with lifetime tenure and the idea of the teacher as a valued and highly trained individual being replaced with a liberalized, business-influenced model of teachers as replaceable assets. In some ways, these challenges are reflective of greater social changes; in others, they are unique to the industry.

In the first part of this chapter, we will examine public primary and secondary education (K–12)—its structure, its governance, current crises, and the effects of government initiatives such as No Child Left Behind and Teach for America. We will look at what is needed to work in this sector, such as licensing, and details of the job such as unions and tenure. We will also look at the state of the labor market in terms of the latest statistics and the official Labor Department outlook.

In the second part, we will look at private K–12 education, including private and parochial schools. This is a small but rapidly growing sector of the market, and one that looks poised to become a significant employer. Political developments such as the growth of charter schools, the school voucher controversy, and the school-choice movement will likely affect it greatly. We will examine the types of private schools, the main brands and players, and how qualifications and job descriptions in such schools differ from the public sector.

In the third part of this chapter, we will look at the outlook for postsecondary education—trade schools, community and junior colleges, and colleges and universities. Though the choice of grouping highly qualified, doctorate holding, tenure-track university professors together with trade-school instructors might seem to be unusual, in reality, when we consider higher education as a labor market, these workers have more in common than it would seem. They possess unique qualifications, their institutions are dependent on grants, outside funding, and student tuition, and they are mainly dependent on peer review for assessment of their skills. Also, administrators of both public and private schools, no matter what their level, are adopting similar philosophies toward labor relations. Unionization and the promise of lifetime tenure are rapidly disappearing in favor of casual labor, such as reliance on adjunct professors.

Finally, we will look at nontraditional options in education career paths—such choices as teaching English abroad, special education, teaching in juvenile detention facilities, corporate trainers, and other such situations. We will also look at the distance-learning industry. Though these professionals are not what one might think of when one imagines a "teacher," they are nonetheless essential to the industry, and the career paths they have chosen provide fulfillment and livelihoods for many—besides, of course, the fact that their services are essential to their students.

Public Education

Public education is, for the most part, governed by local school districts. School districts are unique structures in American democracy, usually distinct from town, city, or state governance but vested with similar powers of taxation and eminent domain. There are exceptions: Hawaii and Puerto Rico are both effectively one large school district, Maryland runs its schools at the county level, and New York has both county and city-level school boards. (The New York City school system is, however, becoming increasingly centralized.) School districts are usually composed of an elected school board and a superintendent who acts as an executive of sorts. In cases of serious student or employee misconduct, the school district can also act as a sort of judicial system—by imposing fines or terminating an employee, for example.

Depending on the state, districts may or may not have jurisdiction over high schools. A *unified* school district usually includes high schools. Several other adjectives can also indicate administrative jurisdictions. *Central*, similar to *unified*, means there is one administration. *Free* is a holdover from the nineteenth century meaning that no tuition is charged, or in New York, that it has administration over more than one school district—a condition usually implied by the word *joint* in the rest of the country. *Independent* is a similarly inconsistently used moniker, meaning that schools can be either across county lines or entirely separate from counties.

Individual states also have departments of education or state education authorities that oversee such details as budgets, standards, and textbook adoption. They also control teacher certification. However, just as at one time local districts wielded a lot more power than they now do, so too are state authorities coming increasingly under federal purview. Initiatives such as No Child Left Behind are mandating high-stakes testing, and tapping into the deep pockets of the U.S. Department of Education comes with the condition that federal guidelines are met. However, state school boards, which are elected offices, can still have a great deal of influence. For instance, in 2005, the state of Kansas' school board conducted a well-publicized and much-debated series of hearings of whether evolution or intelligent design should be taught in Kansas public schools. The school board, which controls curriculum, had a powerful influence on whether or not intelligent design theory should be taught along with, and in opposition to, evolution. Though the proposal was eventually defeated, the affair showcased the significant and continuing power of state education authorities.

The U.S. Department of Education was created in 1979 from the former Department of Health, Education, and Welfare. It is a cabinet-level department, albeit the smallest one. The Department of

Education does not educational create policy, but it does implement it. It is headed by the U.S. Secretary of Education and consists of offices charged with overseeing different aspects of American education—budgets, civil rights compliance, risk management, postsecondary educations standards, student aid, and so on. No Child Left Behind is administrated by the Department of Education. The FICE code, the six-digit identifier for each postsecondary institution that is well-known to anyone who has ever filled out a federal aid application, was created by the Federal Interagency Committee on Education. Similarly, Web sites in the "dot-edu" domain may be obtained only by institutions accredited by a body on the Department of Education's list of approved accrediting bodies. The department currently has a budget of almost $70 billion. It is not immune to criticism; "small-government" conservatives believe government has no business regulating education.

There are also a number of important non-government players in the field. Foremost amongst these are the National Education Association (NEA) and the American Federation of Teachers (AFT), the labor unions that together represent 4.6 million American teachers, former teachers, and support personnel. (According to the Department of Labor, half the teachers in the United States are unionized.) The NEA, with 3.2 million members, is the largest labor union in the United States. These unions advocate for fair pay, just working conditions, and often lobby for or against education-related legislation. Joining the union is mandatory in most public school systems. However, they have been criticized for a historically liberal bias, which means that teachers may have to pay dues to an organization with whose principles they do not necessarily agree. The NEA, for instance, has been accused of lobbying against anything it sees as against the status quo, such as No Child Left Behind, merit pay, and the weakening of teacher tenure. (The other side argues equally vociferously that these interest groups in fact hurt American education.) The New York City branch of the American Federation of Teachers, known as the United Federation of Teachers or UFT, has also been harshly accused of not doing *enough* lobbying, and instead colluding with Mayor Michael Bloomberg's initiatives to run the city schools in a more business-like fashion. (The UFT has also opposed Bloomberg in many circumstances, such as high-stakes testing.)

Academic experts also play a large role in influencing curriculum and pedagogy. The main academic players are Bank Street College of

Fast

Facts

Industry Statistics

Preschool, Kindergarten, Elementary, and Middle School Teachers

Employment (2006): 2.9 million (437,000 preschool; 170,000 kindergarten; 1.5 million elementary school; 674,000 middle school)

Median salary (2006): $43,580 to $48,690

Average salary (2004–2005): $47,602

Occupational outlook: 13 percent growth between 2006 and 2016

Educational Requirements: BA, certification (for public school teachers)

High School Teachers

Employment (2006): 1.1 million

Median salary (2006): $43,580 to $48,690

Average salary (2004–2005): $47,602

Occupational outlook: 5 percent growth between 2006 and 2016

Educational Requirements: BA, certification (for public school teachers)

Education and Columbia Teachers' College in New York, the Erikson Institute in Illinois, Pacific Oaks College in California, and Wheelock College. What this means in practice is that national and local curriculums, as well as classroom emphases, can be developed with the most expert guidance that exists, and that the latest educational research can be incorporated into the most effective pedagogy possible. It also means that academic and social concerns such as respect for diversity can be implemented in the classroom. The negative side is that "flavor of the month" educational ideas and fads trickle down into seemingly illogical directives that might conflict with students' actual needs. Such associations have also been criticized as pushing social and political agendas where they are not wanted.

Postsecondary Teachers

Employment (2006): 1.7 million

Median salary (2006): $56,120

Average salary (2006–2007): $73,207

Occupational outlook: 23 percent growth between 2006 and 2016

Educational Requirements: MA, usually PhD or other terminal degree

Teacher Assistants

Employment (2006): 1.3 million

Median salary (2006): $20,740

Occupational outlook: 10 percent growth between 2006 and 2016

Educational Requirements: BA usually required

Special Education Teachers

Employment (2006): 459,0000

Median salary (2006): $46,360 (primary school); $47,650 (middle school); $48,330 (high school)

Occupational outlook: 15 percent growth between 2006 and 2016

Educational Requirements: BA, licensing

Source: U.S. Department of Labor

Finally, there are corporations such as the Educational Testing Service (ETS), and the College Board. The former administrates such high-stakes tests as the Graduate Record Administration; the latter administers Advanced Placement (AP) tests. Both corporations, which are registered not-for-profits, are jointly in charge of the SAT, with the College Board developing the test and ETS administering it. Besides the usual criticisms of high-stakes testing, critics point to the fact that these companies have a near-monopoly over the futures of millions of would-be college students.

How does this play out in the classroom? States set education standards, which in turn influence what teachers must include in their classroom lesson plans. School administrators both on the level of the individual school (such as principals and vice principals) and on the district level supervise lesson plans, hold teacher training, and ensure that standards are met. The state education departments also set certification standards. Public education is, in short, a very top-down enterprise, with various directives implemented throughout the hierarchy and less and less diversity at the local level being possible. These directives are, in turn, shaped by both political considerations and by the advice of educational experts. The terrain of modern educational is thus a far cry from the locally supported grammar schools that once dotted the American landscape.

National Education Standards

Though state education standards are an old idea, they gained new currency in 2000 when President Clinton and the U.S. Department of Education declared that "all states and schools will have challenging and clear standards of achievement and accountability for all children." In response to this "Goals 2000" initiative, state educational authorities began to implement new state standards for education—clear, specific bullet-pointed goals and requirements—related to the National Education Standards. These standards, in fine arts, language arts, mathematics, physical education and health, science, social sciences, and technology, had in turn been developed by outside bodies of experts, such as the International Society for Technology in Education and the National Association for Sport and Physical Education. These are usually composed of academic leaders in the education sub-fields. They are also historically political battlegrounds. We have already seen the Kansas school board evolution controversy; other examples of areas where liberal academia has met conservative politics are sex education and the "revisionist history" that paints America's expansionist past in a bad light.

Needless to say, like everything designed by committee and influenced by politics, these standards can cause some frustration on the part of the end-user (that is, the teacher). For instance, filling a standard's requirements might require wildly varying parameters. A technology standard might direct something vague, such as "Students develop positive attitudes toward technology uses that support lifelong learning, collaboration, personal pursuits, and productivity" (which is impossible to meaningfully measure) or something more specific, such as "Students use productivity tools to collaborate in constructing technology-enhanced models, prepare publications, and produce other creative works" (in which case students can produce models or publications to show that they have filled the standard). Luckily (or unluckily) for the individual teacher, lesson plans, classroom materials, and means of incorporating standards are usually passed down from above.

It is, of course, impossible to cover every state's specific standards in this book. Since they take into account local history and curriculum variations, they can vary widely. California's health standards are not the same as Arkansas', and students in New York do not learn about Oklahoma's past as Indian Territory in their social studies lessons. However, there is no need to list them all: The standards are published on state Department of Education Web sites, available with a quick Internet search. (Typing in the state's name, subject area, grade level, and "standards" usually produces a good result.)

Unlike NCLB, which is tied to federal monies, these standards are voluntary on the parts of the states—though for the teachers charged with implementing curriculum they are of course *not* voluntary. In practice, they often take up class time better spent on test-preparation and are left by the wayside in response to getting ready for high-stakes testing. Since there is no high-stakes test in music or painting, arts education is often neglected. However, this need not be necessarily so. The example in the accompanying "Problem Solving" sidebar gives one way to incorporate the requirements of disparate material into lesson plans.

There is also a small but growing movement to have national standards at the college level. This is not such a revolutionary idea; European countries such as France have national university examinations. However, it would be a very large change in the way that things are done in America. Currently, colleges and universities are accredited by independent certifying authorities. As recognized experts in their fields, professors are relatively autonomous in what they are allowed to teach, provided it passes the muster of their colleagues. Academic hiring and tenure is also based on the recommendations of colleagues, not supervisors. Peer review, not governmental oversight, is the standard on which higher education is predicated. In February 2008, Charles Spelling, an investor who chaired President Bush's Commission on the Future of Higher Education, was quoted as saying, "What is clearly lacking is a nationwide system for comparative performance purposes, using standard formats." However, such a system for standardized testing and oversight of professors' work is unlikely to be passed in the near future.

Budget Problems

The fact that education is a not-for-profit venture and that its dividends are not obvious to most people makes it a constant target for legislators looking to trim budgets. This is especially true in hard financial times, such as the 2008–2009 recession. Many schools have made ends meet with federal stimulus money. However, it is a fact that schools, especially in poorer areas, perennially have to make do with less. Because low-income areas have lower property values, lower salaries, and lower taxes, but often higher populations densities, there is less money per child available in such areas. Parents tend to be less politically active and tend not to donate money to candidates. Politicians listen to these constituencies less, which means that old or used-up infrastructure is slow to be replaced. Also, parents from more affluent income brackets have the option to move or send their children to private school; to keep them in the system, their local districts must be competitive. Students in low-income neighborhoods thus often have to make do with substandard libraries, crumbling buildings, larger class sizes, and less-experienced teachers.

One way to offset budgetary shortfalls is money from above. The wider an area that money can be collected from—city, state, or national—the more widely it can be redistributed. This is one great advantage of initiatives such as No Child Left Behind: They represent a wellspring of federal money, and these funds are expected to be used to correct imbalances between richer, higher-achieving school districts and those that are poorer and lower-achieving. It also means that lower-achieving schools are held to the same standards as others and not merely allowed to continue failing. Whereas the actual implementation of NCLB is controversial, it does represent one possible answer to economic imbalances between school districts.

Higher education was the hardest hit by the 2008–2009 recession. State schools saw their budgets slashed, and were forced to drop or consolidate programs and even lay off administrative personnel to make ends meet. Many systems, such as the State University of New York, declared hiring freezes, while others, such as the University of Massachusetts–Amherst, overhauled their administrative structures. Private colleges and universities saw the value of their endowments plummet, since they were heavily invested in the stock market. Many have drastically curtailed their financial aid programs. For instance, Reed College, the famous Oregon state

Problem Solving

Incorporating State Standards into Lessons

Let us suppose that John H. is a primary-school teacher in a fictional state somewhere in the United States. His school's pass rates in the statewide NCLB-mandated tests are not as good as they might be; he badly needs all his students to pass the end-of-year test. His students will also be taking a statewide social-studies test concentrating on state history. Furthermore, he has also received a mandate from the state that students must produce work to be displayed on bulletin boards throughout the school. Of course, he also has to teach the usual curriculum of mathematics, science, and other subjects.

John can kill three birds with one stone by creatively combining the three requirements into one. For instance, he can create small multiple-choice tests that replicate the high-stakes state test for his students to take after each social studies reading or lesson. Likewise, rather than simply having students create pictures or collages for the bulletin boards, he can instead assign them to write short reports on various state historical figures that will mirror the sorts of essay requirements they will encounter on the tests. Social studies can thus be used teach language arts.

The same lesson plan can be adapted to fit other requirements, such as small-group discussions. This is a recent trend in which students are given instructions by the teacher and then break up into small groups to solve a problem. Each student can work on part of an essay, or they can fill out the tests cooperatively.

Another example can be combining math and music. Suppose a state standard requires students to explore different counting systems, such as those based on base 4 or base 12. John can have his students count quarter notes, half-notes, and whole notes to see how many bars and measures a particular piece of music will last. He can then show his students how to convert from one cadence to another.

liberal arts college, was forced to drop its need-blind financial policy for the 2009–2010 school year and admit students who could pay rather than students who would have received financial aid. On the other hand, the crisis represented a bonus for less expensive but less prestigious public universities, who are reaping a crop of talented students who would have otherwise gone to private schools.

High-stakes Testing

Modern education is full of so-called "high-stakes testing." We have already mentioned the No Child Left Behind requirements and their effect on the nation as a whole, but testing systems still vary by state. Massachusetts, for instance, has the Massachusetts Comprehensive Assessment System (or MCAS) in English, mathematics, history, and science, while New York has the Regents' exams and California has Standardized Testing and Reporting (STAR). Depending on the state, a high-school diploma can depend on these tests: California has a high-school exit exam and Massachusetts students must pass at least minimal language and mathematics exams to earn their degree. On the other hand, New York awards two diplomas—one Regents and one not. These testing schemes overlap: the Massachusetts MCAS, for instance, fulfills the No Child Left Behind requirements. Most of these tests are mandatory: MCAS must be taken by every student in the Commonwealth of Massachusetts educated with public funds. They are not, however, universal: Many prestigious New York prep schools, arguing that their own standards exceed the state's, do not use the Regents tests.

These tests are called "high stakes" because, much like a poker player who will lose all his money if he is dealt a bad hand, the repercussions for *not* passing are severe for the student. Though such testing has existed for decades, federal initiatives have put a new emphasis on broad, universal testing. For instance, the TAAS, or Texas Assessment of Academic Skills, in which a student only had to pass the grade 10 level in reading, writing, and math to earn a high-school diploma, was replaced in 2003 with the Texas Assessment of Knowledge and Skills (TAKS), in which students must pass proficiency tests in English language arts, social studies, math, and science.

Failure has consequences for educators, as well. As we noted in the last chapter, schools that do not meet NCLB's "Adequate Yearly Progress" two or more years in a row are subject to sanctions, such as mandatory institution of after-school and tutoring programs and parents having the option to transfer their children. Current initiatives are looking at both the carrot and the stick approaches: rewarding teachers for good performance, and firing them for poor performance. Whereas no one disagrees that incompetence in the classroom is a bad thing, teachers have historically been protected from being arbitrarily let go (see discussion of tenure below). Opponents also argue that being able to fire teachers for poor performance would give administrators too much power. Finally, teachers working in underprivileged schools and districts with students in difficult circumstances might be penalized for factors out of their control.

Licensure and Tenure

Every state in the union requires public school teachers to be licensed. Generally, this requires a BA, a sufficient amount of education credits (with a concentration in the field the prospective teacher wants to work in, such as early-childhood education or high school history), a series of interviews, a background check, and the passing of some sort of test. These tests are either the national Praxis test, developed by the Educational Testing Service and used by several states, or a state-specific test developed by Pearson Education. Thanks to the growth of "alternative teaching certification" in the past few decades, would-be teachers do not necessarily need to have completed an undergraduate education major, though there may be additional educational requirements, mentoring, and coursework. Most state systems also require teaching evaluations and student-teaching. Once hired, teachers must also then complete a teaching-based or content-based master's degree (that is, a master's in education or in a subject area) within a certain number of years. They can also gain salary increases for credits over and above the master's degree.

There are exceptions to these licensing requirements. With the growing crisis caused by a shortage of teachers, especially in math and science, programs that bring teachers into schools while they work toward certification have become very popular. This route, known as "alternative certification," first began in the 1980s in response to teacher shortages, but has gained new impetus in recent years. Most prominent is the New Teacher Project, a not-for-profit that works with school districts to attract talented people to the teaching profession who have not prepared with a formal education in pedagogy.

Exact requirements for alternative certification vary by region, but usually involve a short, intensive training course and then studying for certification (taking classes and tests) while actually working in schools. The New York City Teaching Fellows Program is one such program. It places fellows immediately into classroom after pre-service training and taking two legally mandated written tests (the Liberal Arts and Science Test, or LAST, and the appropriate Content Specialty Test, or CST), whereupon they are expected to begin working toward a master's degree. Only then, after two to three years of teaching and earning the degree, are fellows eligible for taking the written Assessment of Teaching Skills test (ATS-W) and earning their initial certification. In other words, no formal New York City requirement is waived—despite the fact that these were designed around those who had not taken the traditional path to the classroom.

The downside is that the pressures of completing academic work toward a master's while teaching sometimes-difficult students in understaffed schools can be exhausting and overwhelming. "In order to complete my master's degree and retain my license, I will have to take an unpaid leave next year, and my school will have to hire a substitute. My tuition will be paid not through a city program, but by a private philanthropist. In other words, I'm lucky," Tom Moore, a New York City teaching fellow, wrote in a 2006 *New York Times* editorial. He noted that the city, while having high expectations of its fellows, did not do enough to support them—thus contributing to a high attrition rate.

On the other hand, the Texas Teaching Fellows program, another New Teachers Project, has a five- to six-week summer training program before placing new teachers in the classroom. They do not have to pay the (minimal) tuition for the teaching program until they are placed in a classroom, and they can earn full certification after one year. The only other requirements are passing the content-knowledge Texas Examinations of Educator Standards (TExES) exam, and passing the Pedagogy and Professional Responsibilities Exam (PPR) by their first year of teaching. The program also requires an undergraduate GPA of 2.75 (or 2.5 with extenuating circumstances); New York City requires a 3.0.

Teach for America (TFA) is another such program. Founded in 1990 by Wendy Kopp with the mission to end educational inequality, TFA has long attracted idealistic young people who are eager to commit themselves to public service. It has since placed 14,000 teachers for a minimum two-year commitment. Like New Teacher Project programs, Teach for America has a rigorous and proven crash course in teacher education. Unlike New Teacher Project programs, Teach for America members often do not complete full certification, but rather enter classrooms. Of course, they do not need to, since the commitment is only two years—though of course, many do complete certification and continue on as regular teachers. Teach for America volunteers also do not get to choose where they will be placed, and may wind up far from friends and family. On the plus side, they get educational vouchers that can be used to pay for college tuition or repay student loans.

Once a teacher is hired, they are usually considered probationary for a few years (usually three). Their work is heavily observed, and they do not have the job protections that regular teachers enjoy. If a probationary teacher is disciplined or threatened with dismissal, the burden of proof is on them to show that the school system is acting in an unfair manner or has the facts of the case wrong. In effect, the teacher works at the pleasure of the school district. This "probationary status" ends, usually after three years, when teachers are granted tenure. Tenure essentially means that a teacher cannot be fired without cause, though what the cause is varies by state. Some justifiable causes are insubordination (that is, refusing to follow orders), gross misconduct such as mistreating a student (which in today's parlance can be anything from a reassuring pat on the arm to sexual assault), or gross incompetence. In effect, tenure means that a teacher cannot be fired without due disciplinary process, which usually is a very involved and difficult thing to do, involving much paperwork and many time-consuming hearings. It is therefore usually not used, save in the gravest circumstances. Usually, quietly transferring the teacher is an easier recourse. Likewise, if layoffs are necessary, teachers are usually let go on the basis of seniority, not performance (barring such exigencies as shortages in one subject or another).

Teacher tenure has been criticized in recent years. Opponents maintain that it rewards laziness and incompetence and penalizes young, energetic teachers. Once tenured, teachers have very little motivation to do much save mark time toward retirement. On the other hand, public-school teaching is a hard job. Half of all new teachers leave within five years. One could argue that perks such as job security are what draw new talent into a field that is otherwise extremely demanding and poorly compensated.

Private Education

Private schools fit into many descriptions, from elite boarding academies such as the Phillips Andover Academy in Andover, Massachusetts, and the Phillips Exeter Academy in Exeter, New Hampshire (both founded by the Phillips family in the late eighteenth century), to humble parochial schools and private education for students with special needs. Montessori and Waldorf schools also usually fit into this category. There are also *charter schools,* which are funded by public monies but are freed from many of the strictures and procedural requirements of public schools (thus, the "charter" they are granted by state-authorized authorities). Charter schools are run both by for-profit companies, such as EdisonLearning, and not-for-profit companies such as Uncommon Schools in New York City. Charter schools are a new and important movement in education, standing midway between public and private schools, and will be considered separately.

Teaching in a private school is appealing to many people for many reasons. Though private school teachers are not unionized and do not have many of the benefits that public school employees enjoy, such as tenure, there are plenty of other perks. To begin with, private school teachers are usually (but not always) seen as better compensated than their publicly employed colleagues. Data on private school compensation is hard to come by, but the National Association for Independent Schools reported an average starting salary of $30,707 for private school teachers in 2002–2003. This may be skewed, however, by the fact that teachers at many religious schools (especially clergy) are paid very little.

A second appealing characteristic is that private school teachers do not usually need to complete the complicated licensing and continuing education credits that states require. This is not to say that no accreditation is required, however. Despite the fact that it is not legally mandated, most schools prefer to hire teachers with state accreditation, and it is a good idea for advancement and for staying marketable. Specialist certification in a subfield such as guidance counseling and prior teaching experience are also good things to have in competing for private-school teaching positions. Some private school organizations, such as the National Association of Private Catholic and Independent Schools (NAPCIS), also have their own accreditation process.

Since many private schools are selective in their admissions, the quality of the students is usually perceived to be higher. Class sizes are also usually smaller—less than half of that of public schools, on average—and private school teachers have more leeway in setting curriculum, or at least more input. Schools are smaller, and the management usually has fewer layers. Rather than being ultimately responsible to thick strata of vice principals, principals, and administrators, all the way up to a viceroy-like superintendent who will not usually know an individual teacher's name or face, a private-school teacher will usually be familiar with all of their supervisors. Finally, private schools want to create ideal teaching environments, not bureaucratic efficiency. This can result in much more pleasant working conditions. For someone with an undergraduate or graduate degree from a good school looking to enter the educational field, teaching in a private school can be an obvious choice.

An important detail to remember when seeking employment in a private school is that as private entities, religious schools are well within their rights to discriminate on the basis of religion. A

On the Cutting Edge

Rewarding Performance

The idea of merit pay is a rather old one. Currently, teachers' salaries are linked solely to job and seniority. Those who teach at the best schools are paid at the same rate as those who teach at the worst. Provable results such as test scores and student outcomes, as well as the difficulty of reaching certain students, are not taken into account.

The arguments for merit pay are many. Americans like the idea that those who do a better job should be rewarded. Teachers offered better pay for better results would also work harder and apply themselves toward a goal. Such pay bonuses would also draw more people, especially talented young people, toward what has historically been an underpaid profession.

On the other hand, exactly how to determine who has earned merit pay, and distributing the money, would be an organizational headache and probably an expensive one. Exactly what "meritorious" results are, and how to measure them (standardized test scores? dropout rates? students going to college? ranking teachers against one another?) is a matter of controversy. Merit pay can also introduce competition and mistrust within a faculty, as well as encourage dishonesty. Finally, teachers would be disinclined to work in disadvantaged schools who did not meet the "merit" standards. The answer, opponents hold, is better pay for all teachers.

Catholic school may only hire practicing Catholics, a Jewish yeshiva may set similar guidelines, and evangelical Christian school might require faculty members to make a profession of faith and inquire into whether a prospective or current teacher meets moral standards of the church in their private life.

Private schools are accredited by one of several organizations, which also function as industry representatives. The largest and most important is the National Counsel for Private School Accreditation, or NCPSA, which serves as an umbrella organization for 13 religious and secular organizations. There are also regional and state accreditation boards, as well as exclusively religious boards such as NAPCIS.

Montessori and Waldorf

Montessori and Waldorf schools are currently big names in the alternative-education industry. As we mentioned in the Chapter 1, the Montessori Method was founded by Maria Montessori (1870–1952) in the late nineteenth and early twentieth centuries. One of Italy's first female physicians, she turned to educational philosophy, espousing the principle that "children teach themselves." Accordingly, Montessori educators act as facilitators or directors, guiding children with carefully constructed materials.

The detail of Montessori education most relevant to industry professionals, however, is the fragmented nature of the Montessori movement. Accreditation is one way in which this comes up: Teachers are trained and accredited by MACTE, the Montessori Accreditation Council for Teacher Education, which is recognized by the U.S. Department of Education; the American Montessori Society; and the Montessori School Accreditation Commission. Montessori principles have also been adopted by more mainstream educators and may be included in standard pedagogical programs. Some states will accept a Montessori-training degree as part of the education required to become a teacher; others will want to see a standard undergraduate education on top of the certification. The best advice on this matter is to ensure that any training you might undertake meets local requirements—or, if you are already certified teacher, that any Montessori training you might have or begin meets the requirements of local schools where you might be employed. Most Montessori organizations are concerned with meeting the NCLB standards; because of state education standards, "teaching to the test" still influences all aspects of education.

Professional Ethics

Balancing Religion and Education

Most religions do not take a stand on most forms of knowledge. Pope John Paul II explicitly stated in his 1990 apostolic constitution *Ex Corde Ecclesiae* ("from the heart of the Church") that "The university community of many Catholic institutions includes members of other Churches, ecclesial communities and religions, and also those who profess no religious belief. These men and women offer their training and experience in furthering the various academic disciplines or other university tasks." But what if a teacher's own conscience and the demands of their employer conflict? How can one teach biology in a school that does not allow evolution to be mentioned, or deal objectively with the Protestant Reformation at a Catholic school, or give a sympathetic account of Muslim beliefs at an evangelical Christian school, or run a debate on gay marriage at an Arabic school, or deliver the sex ed component of a state-mandated health class at a conservative yeshivah? Bear in mind that the students might actively wish to discuss such matters with you; in more closed communities, you might be seen as a link to the outside world.

In such cases, one must remember that the students are attending this particular institution because their parents wish them to be raised in a certain belief system. Your job, when you work for one of these schools, is not to spread your beliefs. Nor is it necessarily to help your employers to spread theirs. Rather, it is to teach your subject. However, you must be respectful of their belief system. That being said, there often is a great deal of leeway; for instance, there are many liberal Catholics who do not agree with the official Vatican stance on many issues.

Finally, if there is something you feel strongly about and that you will not be able to remain silent about, you might reconsider teaching in a religious school.

The educational philosophy of Waldorf schools is based on the work of Rudolf Steiner, an Austrian philosopher and founder of Anthroposophy, a spiritual movement that believes that human beings can achieve knowledge of an objective spiritual world through inner contemplation guided by the scientific method. While this might sound slightly unusual, it has a long connection to a tradition of German and Austrian idealistic philosophy epitomized by the writings of the Georg Wilhelm Friedrich Hegel and Immanuel Kant. Waldorf schools have a high imaginative component, such as playing with the "Waldorf doll," which is intentionally made simple so as to be a blank slate for a child's imagination. Elementary education, including literacy, only begins at seven years of age. Even after the introduction of rigorous academic subjects, Waldorf education contains a high imaginative and artistic component. Waldorf schools tend to disdain standardized tests and textbooks. They also incorporate anthroposophic principles such as a dislikes of antibiotics and sometimes even immunizations; a certain infusion of spirituality; and physical education that includes eurythmy, movement in time to music or the spoken word.

Waldorf schools are independently governed and tend not to have hierarchal organizations, instead being governed by group consensus, though umbrella organizations exist such as the Association of Waldorf Schools of North America (AWSNA). According to their Web site, Whywaldorfworks.org, there are now more than 250 Waldorf schools in the United States, in addition to numerous homeschoolers. The Web site also lists worldwide teacher education programs, most of which lead to certificates in Waldorf education, but some of which lead to an M.S.Ed degree. Waldorf teacher education is a two- or four-year process, depending on if it is undertaken full-time or as summer intensives.

Another alternative that is growing in popularity is the school co-op. This is a middle ground between a private school and homeschooling. Rather than being taught all subjects by one's parents, children in homeschool co-ops come together to learn from adults experienced in one or more subjects, as well as for sports and extracurricular activities. Such co-ops might be religious or secular in nature. They sometimes, but not always, hire outside educators and coaches. (Note that such co-ops differ from *cooperative education*, which blends classroom and work experiences.)

Religious Schools

As we saw in the last chapter, though the first schools were religious, the idea of the nonsectarian free public school was a nineteenth-century innovation. Modern religious schools, such as the parish schools established by Archbishop John Hughes in New York, were established in opposition to this. Other groups, such as Lutherans, also established their own schools.

Due to the Establishment clause of the First Amendment—which guarantees the separation of church and state—religious schools in the United States are invariably private and are called by a variety of names. Some specific terms may be *parochial schools*, that is, Catholic schools run by a parish or diocese; *yeshivahs*, which are run by Jewish organizations; and *Arabic schools*, which are run by Muslim organizations. (The term *madrassa* is generally not used in the United States due to its association with radicalism, while, due to the strong Catholic history in religious education, any religious school may be referred to as a "parochial" school in common usage.) Generally, they teach the state curriculum, plus a variety of other subjects. Language is one example: Muslim students will learn and read the Qua'ran in Arabic; Jewish students will study Hebrew and often Yiddish; Catholic school students will study Latin. Instruction in religion and daily prayer arc other activities that one finds at a religious school. Some are open only to students of a particular faith; others (especially Catholic schools) do not necessarily have a religious test.

Religious schools may be run by either a religious order or a lay board of trustees. As we noted above, working in a religious school does not necessarily mean that one has to profess that particular faith—though administrators often like to see that an applicant has some sort of religious life. Jesuit schools are open to talented instructors from all religions, and yeshivahs (particularly in Yiddish-speaking communities) often hire non-Jewish instructors, especially in English. Nonetheless, hiring preference is often given to those who profess a particular faith.

Charter Schools

Charter schools bridge the line between public and private. Though they have been making headlines recently, they are not a relatively recent idea. They were conceived in the early 1970s by Ray Budde, a professor at the University of Massachusetts–Amherst, and were presented in 1974 in a paper titled "Education by Charter." Budde's idea was for "a four-level line and staff organization" (that is, the various levels of school boards) to be changed to "a two-level form in which groups of teachers would receive educational charters directly

INTERVIEW

Online Teacher

Christine Halem
Online professor, Kaplan University

How long have you been teaching online?
Since 2004. I started full-time in 2006.

What does the job entail?
A lot of people ask me this, and it is a little difficult to explain. It is like a regular classroom, but it is all online. They get assignments, and there are drop boxes. There's synchronous learning, which is like a chatroom using Voice Over IP, and asynchronous, with discussion boards and e-mail drop-boxes. Since I have first-term students, there's also a lot of student support work.

What do you teach?
I teach Academic Strategies, Career Strategies, and Experiential Learning Assessment. The first two are really learning and life skills, while the third is what lets us give academic credit for life experience—it is applying academic skills to your life learning.

What is your educational and career background?
I have a master's degree in English literature, I have almost a master's

from the school board." In other words, management was to be local instead of regional. The idea of the charter school began to be implemented in Minnesota, and was embraced by the American Federation of Teachers in 1988, but in so doing, it has undergone some important changes. The foremost of these is that instead of using existing buildings and infrastructure, new charter schools have been built. The second is that, rather than the individual school-by-school management, with teachers deciding curriculum emphases and pedagogical methods and in return taking responsibility for students' success, charter schools have been heavily influenced by standards-based education and high-level oversight.

Charter schools may be run by different types of organizations and receive their mandates from the state, the local school board, or

degree from Columbia (37 credits) in Continuing Education, and I'm doing another master's at Kaplan, an online master's, in higher education administration.

How did you get into online teaching?
By fluke, actually. I used to work for Kaplan test prep, and I was their vice president of training and development. One of the executives transferred to Kaplan University and he asked me to come down to Florida to help start the Center for Teaching and Learning.

What are the ups and downs of teaching online?
I think that when you teach online, you are more available to your students. When you teach in a classroom, they expect to see you twice a week. Online, they are not shy about speaking up. That's one of the biggest differences I've noticed between in-person and online teaching—and online, they tell you all sorts of things that I do not think they'd tell you face-to-face. Also, my students are from all over the country and even the world. I've had soldiers in Iraq and Afghanistan. I even have a sailor on a ship—she's in Hawaii, last I spoke to her!

What is your advice to anyone wanting to get into online teaching?
My first response is do it. I would say that you have to be willing to be very available, and if that's something you like, that is, being involved with your students beyond the academic realm, then that's something for you.

the district. They are autonomous public schools—that is, they are not subject to district interference (and sometimes even union agreements), and they may not charge tuition. They are also accountable for student performance. To date, approximately 4,000 charter schools have been founded. Almost 90 percent have been successful; the rest closed because of management or financial problems, or sometimes consolidation or direct interference.

The management of a charter school may be a for-profit or not-for-profit corporation, an academic institution, or even a school district. For-profit corporations may only run a charter school in several states—California, Arizona, Wisconsin, and Michigan. Edison-Learning, Inc. (formerly Edison Schools) is the best-known example of the former. Though once praised by free-market capitalists for

their promise to run schools better and more efficiently, for-profit charter-school companies have been harshly criticized: According to the National Education Association, they do not outperform not-for-profit schools, and funds that might otherwise go to students are instead funneled to shareholders. Edison, for instance, has never made a profit; and today, after reorganization, only manages a handful of schools and instead concentrates on providing services to the educational industry.

Not-for-profits are a different story. They are usually motivated by idealism. New York City-based Uncommon Schools, for instance, is a charter management organization (CMO) with the explicit mission of preparing underprivileged students to graduate from college. They currently run close to a dozen charter schools in New York and New Jersey, with plans to more than double that number throughout the Northeast.

Some studies have found that charter schools do tend to improve test scores, while others have found little or no difference. The counterargument is that students who tend to apply for and attend charter schools tend to come from more affluent backgrounds with parents who take an active interest in their educations. (Admissions to charter schools tend to be by lottery.) The effectiveness of charter schools over other sorts of schools is debated. What is most important, perhaps, is that they cut out much of the state bureaucracy and involve communities in the process of education their children.

There has been a lot of discussion lately about the issue of school vouchers. Simply put, an education voucher is money given to a family for their child to attend a school of their choice, rather than their assigned public school. School choice is an important concept in educational reform. Proponents argue that school vouchers will create a free market in education, rather than subsidizing private schools. Given a free market and open competition, the best schools will thrive and the worst will fail. It also gives parents more control over their children's education, and means that those who opt out of public schools will not be penalized by having to pay taxes to support them in addition to private school tuition.

Opponents such as the teachers' unions argue that vouchers would destroy public education. The funding base would be undercut, standards would be eroded, and teachers would leave public schools in droves. Due to the belief that private schools offer better educations (a belief contested by the opponents of vouchers),

competitive private schools would be able to "skim" the best students, while the rest would be left to languish in substandard public education.

One area of controversy is if a voucher, which is, after all, public funds raised through taxes, could be paid to a private religious school. Opponents have argued that this would violate the separation clause of the First Amendment, since the government would, in effect, be paying for religious education. In 2002, the Supreme Court decided in the case *Zelman v. Simmons-Harris* that vouchers could indeed be used in sectarian schools.

Finally, it should be noted that one circumstance in which vouchers are routinely given is when a school fails standards such as those established under No Child Left Behind. In *Zelman v. Simmons-Harris*, for instance, vouchers were given because the Cleveland public schools were deemed failures and the state of Ohio gave parents vouchers that could be used in both public and private schools.

Postsecondary Education

American colleges and universities are currently facing a crisis of sorts. This is both budgetary and in terms of mission. Whereas the idea of higher education originated in providing a liberal education for the upper class, since World War II it has become increasingly oriented toward practical studies. This trend has accelerated in recent years thanks to new management principles and budget crises. As a *New York Times* headline summed it up, "In Tough Times, Humanities Must Justify Their Worth." (A market-based counterargument is that medieval history or philosophy or literature are all valuable and important because people want to study them.)

Furthermore, the master's is, in many ways, the new bachelor's degree. With the new ubiquity of the BA, people feel that they need another sign that they are truly educated. An MA indicates that one can reason, write, is intellectually curious, wants to learn new things, and can see a project through. However, personal enrichment is not the aim of graduate study; rather, the ostensible aim of an advanced degree is "professionalization" —that is, indoctrination into the norms of the academic discipline. The forms and goals of graduate school in both the liberal arts and the sciences (as opposed to professional degrees such as the MBA), from first-year seminars to research work, are geared toward producing the next generation of professors. However, even though older professors speak of someone "leaving the profession" in the same way that normal people speak of an untimely death, those who do not wind up in academia can still pursue other avenues. As one medieval historian who left the ivory tower noted, "As a humanities PhD, I can take a massive amount of confusing information, sift out what's important, and present it in a coherent way." This is something no computer, and an awful lot of supposedly educated people, cannot do, and which employers find valuable. Nonetheless, there is increasing concern that the increase in graduate education is causing a "bubble economy" of sorts.

But what about those who *do* want to become college professors? To begin with, the way is long and hard, since a PhD is the minimum requirement for employment at most colleges and universities. (Two-year schools will often employ instructors with MAs, but will want to see other experience, especially in teaching, and some schools will hire graduate students who are "All But Dissertation," or ABD, with the promise that they will finish their degrees within a reasonable amount of time.) Yet, despite the obstacles and the difficult job market, graduate programs continue to fulfill their intended function of training new PhDs. Thus, there is a relative oversupply of labor versus available positions. Though the Department of Labor continues to project a high rate of growth in the field, the promised baby boomer retirements have never materialized, and college administrators, working with the same logic as corporate human resources, have outsourced as much labor as possible to a hungry pool of adjunct, or part-time, professors who will work for less money and no benefits. Wages are thus kept low, especially in disciplines where private industry is not competing for labor (such as history and political science, versus psychology and engineering, for example).

Of course, there will always be a need for tenure-track professors, since a demand exists for degrees and adjuncts cannot teach graduate seminars or supervise MA theses. More people going to grad school in the humanities—even if they are only going to teach high school or are taking a year or two between their bachelor's and law school—means more jobs for those who do want to make academia a career. However, to land such a job, the conventional wisdom is that you will need a PhD from a top-tier program and a considerable number of publications and grants on your curriculum vitae.

Other current events are also shaking up academia. During the 2008–2009 recession, most public universities had their budgets slashed as states lost tax revenue, and private schools saw the

Professional Ethics

Do Not Assume Things about Your Students!

Mandy F. was an adjunct professor at Anystate College. Like many state schools, Anystate admits a wide variety of students, including some that were not prepared for college-level work. Mandy found herself having to fail a fairly large percentage of her students each semester, and often despaired of her students' poor writing and reasoning skills.

In addition to her classroom teaching duties, Anystate paid Mandy to teach an online course in her subject area. She noted that they seemed to think of their online coursework in the same idiom as text messages, and she wished they would pay more attention to proper English style and usage.

One of Mandy's students was particularly egregious, responding to discussion-forum threads and required assignments with one- or two-sentence replies that were remarkable for their lack of grammar and spelling and occasionally being typed entirely in capital letters. Mandy wasn't surprised when her student withdrew from the course and sent what she thought was a considerate, thoughtful e-mail expressing regret that the work had proven too much for her and hoping that she would have luck finding remedial writing and try the course again in the future.

As it turned out, her student did not consider herself to be ill-prepared for college—she was a single mother who worked at the school and was having difficulty balancing her professional, academic, and family lives. In fact, she took great offense at Mandy's e-mail and complained to the dean. She was also politically well-connected and in a position to make a great deal of trouble for a lowly adjunct professor. Needless to say, Mandy's contract was not renewed for the following semester. All of this goes to show that in the online world, one cannot assume anything about his or her students, and that each one needs to be treated with the same patience, courtesy, and respect as would be expected in a "brick-and-mortar" classroom environment.

investment portfolios in which they had invested their endowments shrink—by an average of 20 percent, according to some sources. Many positions that would have otherwise been filled are remaining vacant, and some statewide university systems put hiring freezes in effect. Whether or not these positions will be filled when the economy improves, or whether departments will have to do more with less, remains to be seen.

Community colleges are a career opportunity for those who cannot, or do not want to, teach at a four-year school. To begin with, the number of community colleges, and their enrollment, is expanding exponentially. They can be very comfortable places to work, with tenure and low publishing demands. On the other hand, the pay can also be relatively low, and the teaching load quite high.

Other Educational Markets

There are many other career paths in education that do not fit neatly into the three large categories of public school teaching, private school teaching, and higher education. For adventuresome educators, these can provide not just job satisfaction, but also a broad range of life experiences.

One possibility is teaching abroad. Military bases, diplomatic missions, and foreign boarding schools often hire English-language teachers, especially those with verifiable certification. In higher education, programs such as George Soros' Open Society Institute and the Fulbright program send American academics abroad every year. Likewise, many foreign universities feel that American university degrees are more prestigious, and are eager to hire graduates, even those with only an MA. Many expatriates also support themselves by teaching English, a skill that is in demand throughout the world. In this case, it is greatly useful to obtain TEFL (Teaching English as a Foreign Language) certification, as well as to speak the language of the country where you want to go. Because teaching abroad is not tracked by the U.S. Department of Labor, it can be hard to get statistics on how many people follow this career path.

Another possibility is teaching in juvenile facilities, institutions, and group homes. This can be a challenging work environment. Getting to your classroom may involve passing through metal detectors and locked gates. Your students might be working on their GED, or not even have learned to read yet. These are young adults who are in need of education, life skills, and a positive direction in life. Trying to reach these most difficult students can be frustrating, but also rewarding.

Teaching in a juvenile detention center at least nominally requires the same teaching credentials as in any other school. However, such teachers are less likely to be certified and, due to the lack of volunteers willing to take the job, this may be overlooked. They are also often less experienced. It is not necessarily a dangerous job; these are, after all, high-security areas. However, it can be stressful and frustrating.

Finally, the Internet is changing the way we learn today. As noted in the Chapter 1, distance learning has a long history. However, thanks to the Internet, online learning has taken this experience to new levels, and schools such as the University of Phoenix are revolutionizing how people earn their degrees. No longer is a classroom or campus necessary. Such learning can be synchronous, that is, a "virtual class" that meets live at a regular time; or asynchronous, that is, where course materials and assignments are posted to a bulletin board and students and instructors upload their materials. Teaching online can be a blessing in that one is not connected a physical classroom, but it also requires the professor to be more of a self-starter, to be able to turn out large amounts of instructional material. It usually pays less, as well.

Chapter 3

On the Job

This chapter provides a detailed survey of the many positions available in the field of education, focusing on the three main pedagogical levels where one can choose to focus: primary and secondary; postsecondary; and adult, continuing, and professional education.

Primary and Secondary Education (Pre-K–12)

Working at the primary and secondary levels is a true opportunity to instill a lifelong love of learning in your students. This is the stage where their learning habits, interests, and personalities are coming into being, and the need for support and guidance from devoted teachers, administrators, and other educational professionals is absolutely crucial.

Academic Administrator (Private)

Private school administrators come from many backgrounds. Some are idealists who want what is best for children, and see private schools as the best way of doing so. Some have trained specifically for the profession. Some are academics that have fallen into primary and postsecondary teaching. Others are religious men and women with a calling to teach.

Because of the diversity of private schools, it is hard to give an exact rundown of what is required. One school might want a senior member of a religious order; another might require prestigious academic credentials such as a PhD. Some have backgrounds as teachers or as prominent educators or theorists in a particular educational philosophy (Montessori, for instance). Others have gone to school for administration. Not all private schools require a master's degree, as most public systems do. Some, like Waldorf schools, do not even have professional administrators. However, education is usually your best path to employment and advancement.

Like their public school counterparts, private school academic administrators are in charge of running the school. In many private schools, there is an additional element of parental and/or alumni relations involved—both of which are a school's lifeblood. On the other hand, they usually do not have to worry about state or federal directives (though continuing a school's certification may be a concern). Another big difference is unionization: As private schools are not often unionized, administrators do not usually belong to unions. Also, though they are not responsible to the district superintendent, they tend to answer to school trustees or a board of directors (in addition to any religious authorities who might be involved). As with public school administration, there is also often a degree of politicking involved.

In terms of advancement, private school administrators can move up amongst various levels—from assistant headmaster to headmaster, for instance—or take jobs with larger or more prestigious schools. Some, with enough prestige or backing, can even start their own schools.For an excellent guide to some of the challenges you might face, see the Survival Guide for Iowa School Administrators at http://resources.sai-iowa.org.

Academic Administrator (Public)

Educational administrators are the managers of the academic world. Their duties include everything from supervising teachers and setting standards to drawing up schedules, monitoring students' academic progress and test scores, to dealing with budgets and supplies and making sure that the school is safe, orderly, and well-run. An administrator must multitask: He or she might be simultaneously in charge of filing all the medical waivers for a school's athletic teams, career and college counseling, and hiring a new English teacher. Besides all this, he or she will also supervise classroom teaching, fill out performance reviews, set up continuing teacher training, and meet with parents, school board members, and other members of

Professional Ethics

Bad Touch!

The time was when an unruly or ill-behaved child might find themselves being caned, whipped, or spanked by an authority figure. Corporal punishment is still legal in 21 states, and, according to the ACLU, frequently used in 13: Missouri, Kentucky, Texas, Oklahoma, Arkansas, Louisiana, Mississippi, Alabama, Georgia, South Carolina, North Carolina, Tennessee, and Florida. (The Center for Effective Discipline estimates that 223,000 students were physically chastised in 2006.) This is usually done ceremoniously in the principal's office with a paddle. Private schools may also use corporal punishment. However, it is not the individual teacher's place to administer such discipline, and, in fact, it is safer for your career and life to stay far away from it. In New York City, for instance, *any* touching of a student, even accidental, can be considered corporal punishment and is cause for dismissal.

Added to this is the danger of "inappropriate touching." It seems that every day, the media gleefully reports another student-teacher sex scandal. Whether or not the accusations are founded is usually not an issue: In the name of "protecting the children," prosecutors are liable to press charges first and inquire into the facts later. Even if the accused is able to fight the charges, lives and careers can be ruined. Furthermore, such contact need not be overtly sexual in nature: *Any* physical contact can be construed as "inappropriate touching."

Due to all of this, as well as the litigious nature of our society, the moral of the story is clear: Never physically touch a child unless not doing so will clearly result in physical injury or other harm to the child, yourself, or a bystander. If a child touches *you* (for instance, offering a hug), explain that such behavior is inappropriate in such a way that any witnesses can clearly understand that the affection was unwanted.

the community. Responsibilities extend both upward and downward: If a directive comes from on high, it is the administrator who must implement it, while at the same time, he must pass back reports on attendance, disciplinary incidents, finances, and other such matters.

The head manager of a public school is, of course, a *principal*. There are also vice principals, deans, and other administrators. (We will exclude college presidents and school superintendents from this description, as those who fill these executive-like positions often have different backgrounds, different responsibilities, and are compensated at a higher level.) The biggest changes to the job in recent years are the increase in responsibility of individual principals, especially insofar as high-stakes testing goes. Also, as budgets have become tighter, many administrators have been forced to allocate resources more tightly and even turn to the community to make up shortfalls (for instance, asking for donations of athletic equipment). The job is year-round: during the summer, administrators oversee summer school and plan for the coming year.

The process of becoming an administrator varies by school system. One might be a longtime teacher who is promoted to fill a vacancy either temporarily or permanently; another might have followed a separate management track. An assistant principal (AP) might train to become a principal in his own right, or remain an AP for his or her entire career. Generally, public school administrators have master's degrees or even doctorates in education administration or educational leadership, which are accredited through the National Council for Accreditation of Teacher Education (NCATE) or the Educational Leadership Constituent Council (ELCC). This generally includes courses in law, finance and budgets, curriculum developments, politics, counseling, and research design and analysis. Most states also require licensure and a master's degree, though there is also on-the-job training.

To advance, you will have to prove yourself a competent, confident, and results-producing leader. You will also need to know how to play the political game and gain community approval. In time, an educational administrator might rise to the same position in a larger, wealthier, or otherwise more desirable district; to a superintendent's post; or even to educational positions in local, state, or national government.

Administrative Staff (K–12)

It takes more than teachers to make a school run. It also takes secretaries, accountants, and other administrative staff. Such staff may work in the schools themselves, or in district offices. They are frequently unionized, along with the other employees of the school system.

While the educational bar to entering such positions is low (often no more than an associate's degree), advancement opportunities are not often great. In such cases, to go upwards in seniority and status, you will need to improve your credentials. In other cases (such as accountants and other professionals), you will need the usual degree and state accreditation. One potential direction for upward movement is from the school level to the district and, ultimately, the state level. You may also want to change from a low-paying public school job to one at a private school.

Administrator (Pre-K)

The child care needs for working adults with young children are often met by private or public school programs. Many of these operations are very small. In such cases, the owner or director is often the only administrator, in charge of hiring and firing, seeing the facility meets standards, overseeing safety and daily activities, keeping records and payroll, as so on.

In most states, those who run pre-K facilities must be certified. In some cases, this means that they have at least a BA; in others, an associate's degree suffices. Other credentials include general preschool education credentials such as the Child Development Associate (CDA) sponsored by the Council for Professional Recognition or the National Administration Credential, offered by the National Child Care Association, which requires experience and training in child care center management.

Generally, these businesses are independently owned and operated. Administrators are usually more concerned with keeping the doors open and doing a good job than in upward advancement. Those who tire of the stress of owning their own business, however, might be employed by larger facilities or public or private schools.

Instructional Coordinator

An instructional coordinator, also known as a curriculum specialist, personnel development specialist, instructional coach, or instructional material director, handles the "big picture" aspects at the district or state level: buying textbooks, setting curricula, training teachers, finding and implementing new ideas and procedures, and field-testing the same. They also ensure that standards and requirements are being fulfilled, and that instruction is uniform and of sufficient quality throughout the district or area served. The job requires a knowledge of not only local and state laws and regulations, but also federal requirements. At the postsecondary level, instructional coordinators might work with employers and industry organizations to ensure that colleges and universities are turning out graduates with the requisite skills and to make sure their schools' programs remain accredited.

To become an instructional coordinator, one must usually have a master's degree, usually in education or a relevant field; doctorates are usually preferred. It is also common for instructional coordinators to have multiple degrees, including degrees in a particular subject and in education or in the teaching of a particular subject (such as social studies or science education). One must work well with people: Not only can the job get rather political, but it requires polling instructors and conducting focus groups, consulting with experts, and hours of committee meetings and advisory groups. Despite the additional requirements, this can be a lucrative field and represents a possible upward career path for a teacher or administrator. On the downside, one very seldom gets to have classroom contact with actual students.

Large adoptions of textbooks or other pedagogical materials represent lucrative contracts for the big corporations that create these products, and instructional coordinators are often wooed by publishing companies seeking a larger market share. It is very important to remain unswayed by the efforts of industry representatives and to do one's job impartially and professionally. Not only do students deserve the best materials they can get, but even the appearance of impropriety can reflect badly and erode public trust in the state educational system. At the same time, it is important not to be swayed by the latest philosophy or trend in education. While there is only so much one can do about federal or state laws, one must, at the same time, exercise one's discretion and common sense before upending the tried-and-true way that teachers have done things for years.

Librarian

The primary-, middle-, or high-school librarian's jobs differs from the university or public librarian's in some important respects. To begin with, in 25 states the public-school librarian must be a certified teacher. Fourteen states also require a master's degree—either an MLS or another equivalent degree.

School librarians have several important tasks. Of course, they are in charge of ordering, circulation, cataloguing, and all aspects of maintenance—often having to take charge of the many tasks for which a university library would have different employees, or even different departments. Also, to a much greater extent than their public or university counterparts, school librarians are tasked with overseeing information technology and media. Drawing up lesson plans, showing students how to use computers and do research on the Internet, and teaching teachers to implement new technology in the classroom are all part of the twenty-first century school librarian's job description. Making sure that computer use is appropriate also comes under his or her purview.

Teaching is also an important part of the job. It is the school librarian who is charged with ensuring students' basic information literacy. Planning such lessons means coordinating with teachers to come up with projects and to find out each class's needs. One group might need to learn the Dewey Decimal System; another, how to effectively search on the Internet; a third, how to use reference materials for a report. In a very real way, these students' future academic success hinges on a school librarian doing their job well.

Finally, the school library is a safe haven and a quiet place for students to study and read. Unlike in college, public-school students must be supervised every moment of every day. The school, after all, acts "in loco parentis" and is liable for anything that might happen. Yet, schedules in junior high and high school often have gaps and free periods. Many students prefer to use their free periods in the library, catching up on schoolwork or reading. The librarian must maintain good order, ensure that the library is used appropriately, and make sure that it does not become a haven for students cutting class.

Opportunities for advancement are few. One can rise to a supervisory position at a district or even state level, or transfer to a bigger or better school. However, for most school librarians, job satisfaction is in helping young people learn, not in wealth and power—though of course, like all teachers, school librarians receive regular pay raises and benefits.

Music Educator

In this age of standardized and outcomes-based education, music education is a much-neglected but nonetheless important field. Music educators not only teach the next generation of budding Yo-Yo Mas, but instill a lifelong love of music in children.

Music educators in the primary schools must usually have at least a BA in music education, as well as the necessary certifications and credentials. (Those who teach music at the university level are better grouped with postsecondary teachers below.) Today, many work not for school systems, but as consultants who are brought in from the outside. They must have good organizational skills to put together concerts and performances, good scheduling skills to fit in music classes around the rest of a school's schedule, and good teaching skills to fill sometimes less-than-enthusiastic children with interest for Bach and Rachmaninoff. Some very lucky music educators work in specialized performing-arts schools, either public or private; these educators are usually very accomplished in their own rights and graduate from prestigious programs.

Paraprofessional

Paraprofessionals, also called para-pros, instructional assistants, teacher's aides, teacher assistants, or classroom assistants, are so-named because, though they work in the classroom and help narrow the student-teacher ratio, give each child individual and often specialized attention, and help keep an eye on the youngest students, they are not certified teachers. Rather, they complete a course that can be as little as a two-year associate's degree. Some "paras" and teacher assistants are teachers in training; for others, this is a way to make money as a part-time job. Like teachers, No Child Left Behind mandates that paras be "highly qualified," though the definition of this is left to the individual states.

Paras are used in a variety of settings. Most relevantly, they can be used as part of a personalized care plan in special education to help supervise and give extra attention and help to children with learning, mental, behavioral, or emotional difficulties. They may provide one-on-one tutoring if no teacher is available. They can help with technology, act as translators, and deal with parents. They may supervise children during lunch to give regular teachers a break. In some areas, they may be used as substitutes to fill in for a certified teacher for the rest of the year. Some jobs, such as special education, may require additional certifications. Others may require you only to pass an examination. Paraprofessionals work closely with teachers—often under direct supervision. They may also work with administrators, librarians (especially if helping with technology centers), and other workers.

Keeping
in Touch

Networking Opportunities

Networking is key in any industry. This is true for education, as well. Often, it is not what you know, but who you know, that gets you the job or promotion.

Public schools are often intimately tied up with local politics. In these cases, it can be very useful to volunteer for local political campaigns. If the town or neighborhood in which you live always goes the same way in elections, then you are relatively safe in determining who to work for. It is also relatively easy to find out who the local bigwigs are and to help them on their campaigns by stuffing envelopes, canvassing, carrying petitions door-to-door, and other such tasks. Even if you do not live in one of the regions where an elected school board is powerful, this is a good way to get in your *quid pro quo* quota. Other ways of networking in public education are taking classes, doing volunteer work, and attending training.

Professional conferences are another way to meet people, especially for the postsecondary teacher. Though very often your tenure and promotion will be controlled by colleagues who are in your discipline but know little about your exact field, this is a good way to come up with new projects and meet influential people in your own specialty, which in turn can help your scholarly reputation. Another way to do this is the committee work or volunteer administrative work that all academics have to do, but which can, if done correctly, really bring you to the attention of the powers that be. (Conversely, seeming too upwardly mobile or having an unpopular agenda can also render you anathema to your colleagues!)

Usually, networking opportunities are easy to realize. The trick is taking them! Never pass up the opportunity to meet someone new, and remember that people are more inclined to hire those they know personally than to strangers.

From being a paraprofessional, there is nowhere to go but up. You can gain additional education and certification and become a regular certified teacher, or even go into administration. Any other specialty, such as physical education or substitute teaching, is also open to you. In such cases, paraprofessionals have a wealth of experience to draw on, and may be looked at more favorably than someone who has just completed school but has no other experience.

Physical Education Teacher

We all have memories of gym class at school. Perhaps you even played on a team or competed in an individual sport. No matter whether you found physical education to be heaven or hell, it seems like the coach has the easy job: They get to play games for a living. But being a physical education teacher is a lot more than wearing sweatpants, blowing whistles, and yelling a lot.

To begin with, a physical education teacher needs to have a four-year degree in their subject, which involves kinesiology, exercise physiology, and health and wellness. They must also know first aid and CPR, besides the rules and skills for a whole range of sports and games. Some sports, such as fencing, have national certifying bodies for their coaches. These organizations provide endorsements of a coach's ability to teach a particular sport safely and well. It is also important to know about the "new PE," which emphasizes developmentally appropriate (or in some cases, even non-competitive) forms of physical activity.

Physical education teachers need to keep fit themselves. It is hard to be a credible sports and health expert when you are out of shape! Also, the job involves being on your feet a lot. They must know how to motivate children and teenagers who would rather chat and text their friends than play sports, and also be comfortable talking about health and health issues such as sexuality, since teaching these classes is usually their responsibility.

In terms of upward mobility, PE teachers may become full-time coaches or move to positions of more responsibility in bigger schools. (In some parts of the country, being a high school football coach is the next best thing to being the town mayor.) Interestingly, many also move into administration and become principals.

Preschool Teacher

Teaching the youngest children takes a certain personality. One must be patient, caring, and attentive. Dealing with a room full of four-year-olds on a daily basis can be immensely stressful, not to mention messy and tiring. Yet, at the same time, these children rely on the skills that you instill in them for their future academic success. This is a heavy burden, and one not to be shouldered lightly.

Preschool teachers work for both private and public institutions, though there is a higher ratio of private schools and day-care centers in this field than in other age ranges. Preschool involves learning and structured activities. Preschool teachers use play, music, dance, and other means to further children's language and social development. There are no state curriculum standards, however, and the level and quality of the instruction varies widely. Generally, more expensive private preschools both pay better and demand more qualified teachers to provide a higher level of structured activity and instruction.

Meeting state standards is very important. Preschool teachers must be certified in every state and the District of Columbia. This means at least a two-year degree in early childhood education, though many teachers have more. There has been a lot of media attention lately about sub-par day care centers, so state inspectors have been equally busy. One must therefore be careful to keep everything up to code and work carefully to ensure compliance.

Preschool teachers are often the first to identify a learning or behavioral disorder in a child. They therefore must work closely not just with parents and administrators, but with school psychologists, counselors, and other personnel. They must also be able to implement any needed remediation. Ensuring that a child gets the right start to their academic career is the most important thing of all.

There are various roads to advancement for a preschool teacher. One can, of course, always improve one's education and level of certification and move to a bigger or better school. One can also become a supervisor or even open a private preschool of one's own. Administrative posts are also a possibility, as are a variety of independent consulting jobs. Finally, with a doctorate in early childhood development, one can even teach future preschool teachers oneself!

Teacher (Primary or Secondary)

Primary school teachers are what comes to mind when one hears the word "teacher": A man or woman in front of a classroom full of eager young minds. The primary school teacher educates, shapes, and inspires students. Part of the task of the primary school teacher is not only to begin students' education, but also to acculturate them to the norms of the educational system—to instill in them the values and habits that will make them effective learners in high school and college. You are also responsible for their well-being and emotional and social development. This is no small responsibility.

Many of the same job caveats and descriptions apply to high school teachers as to primary-school teachers, with the exceptions that they deal with teenagers (and all the problems and joys that implies) and teach subject areas rather than single classes. Obviously, we cannot cover all the details of this career here; entire academic careers have been made in studying the smallest details of pedagogy and how to best teach children. However, some details of the work environment bear repetition.

First, teachers work closely with both parents and administrators. Public schools, of course, have a long chain of command, all the way from the secretary of education to state departments of education to local superintendents to principals to teachers. If you are in a private school, you can expect a shorter organizational chart, with ultimate responsibility usually resting in headmaster or board of trustees. Charter schools also tend to be independently run, with an organizational tree that tends to be much smaller. Some private schools, especially Waldorf schools, are governed by councils of teachers.

Children's first teachers, however, are their parents. The importance of involving parents in the educational process cannot be overstated. Conversely, when parents are apathetic or disengaged, children, in turn, tend not to take school too seriously. While in some communities, disinterested parents are more the exception than the norm, in others, the situation is sadly the reverse. What must be realized is that even if, in some situations, this generation is lost to the educational system, we can instill attitudes in them that will lead to greater success for their children—responsibility, foresight, and planning.

Teaching has one of the highest dropout rates of any profession, with the U.S. Department of Education estimating that one-third leave after three years and 50 percent of teachers leave after five years. Those who remain are in it for the long haul. They take pride and joy in teaching children for their entire careers, and look forward to regular pay raises and generous retirement benefits. If you are ambitious or just not happy, though, there are options. One can always change from the public to the private sector or vice versa, or look for a job at a more prestigious school in a better area. You could transfer into academic administration. It is also possible, if one has a PhD in education or a similar subject, to teach future educators, or to become an educational consultant or work for a private industry (at a textbook publishing company, for instance). Others leave the educational field entirely, finding jobs in other industries.

Another question is who to go to if you have a problem or question. One might think that going directly to the administration might be the best bet. Usually, though, it is not. Besides the fact that you do not want to be thought of as the squeaky wheel, by making any problem or concern official, all sorts of bureaucratic processes may be set in motion—processes that can be embarrassing down the road and that can be hard to stop. The best thing to do, usually, is confide in an experienced, older colleague who you trust. This way, you cannot only get impartial advice, but talk out the ramifications of a variety of actions and see if the situation has come up before. If the problem is dealt with by your union's contract (such as unpaid work, leave time, or prep periods), it might be wise to go to your union representative. Union reps can work as a buffer between administration and teachers, and shield you against unwanted repercussions. Remember that school systems are, above all, bureaucracies, and do things according to their own logic. As a new teacher, you need to learn the rules of the game and play by them. Accommodation is the word of the day.

School Counselor

It is an old joke, but one that conceals a certain amount of truth: "If you know so much about careers, why did you become a guidance counselor?" The answer is that those who undertake this career path—more properly called a *school counselor*—must have a firm commitment to the mental well being and future academic and career success of the children and teenagers in their charge. School counselors do far more than just provide college-admissions advice: They are listening ears, helpful advice, and occasionally a warning voice reminding teenagers that one needs to think about the future. College and career choices are thus only a small part of the role played by a counselor. They might counsel a depressed or anxious teenager, report child abuse, call a parent in for a conference, administer a test, or refer a case to an outside psychologist or psychiatrist. They must also have a careful knowledge of their rights and duties: When must parents or child protective services be called?

School counselors' responsibilities differ by the age of the students they deal with. At the elementary level, their concerns are mainly students' developing basic social and academic skills, personal development, and any disabilities or learning problems that might arise. Students' emotional well-being is also a concern. At the middle school level, counselors begin to concentrate more on college readiness and career plans, while also being careful to shepherd their charges through the trials and tribulations of adolescence. In high school, college planning takes on an even larger role—which school is right for each student's academic and financial situations, maximizing their chances of admission, and backup choices. All students should have some idea of their future career preferences to shape their thinking, even if they might change their minds in the future; for those who will not go on to college, what vocational training or trade school is right for them?

These can be hard decisions. When one is dealing with motivated students and forward-thinking families, the job is greatly simplified. However, many teenagers do not think about the day after tomorrow, let alone the rest of their lives. Such students must be cajoled into putting some thought into their plans for future. You must also deal with hard cases such as teen pregnancy, substance abuse, and sexual and emotional abuse.

School counselors require significant training. The must usually have a master's degree in counseling from an accredited program. These are certified by the Council on the Accreditation of Counseling and Related Educational Programs (CACREP). State certification is also usually required. Many states require state teaching certification and experience. You can see why becoming a "guidance counselor" is something that requires a real commitment to students' well being and future happiness! You must also genuinely like and be able to communicate easily with children and teenagers. Despite this, there is a huge attrition rate amongst school counselors: Almost two-thirds drop out within two years.

Coordinating with other teachers and administrators is essential. What problems does a student have? How can they improve their schoolwork? A trained observer's opinion counts for much. After all, a school counselor cannot see every aspect of a student's social and academic life.

Opportunities for advancement within the school counseling profession are few. One can always move up to a supervisory or administrative lesson, either at the school level or the district or state level. It is also possible to take a better-paid or more responsible position at a private school. Private industry and counseling are also viable alternatives; independent college and career counselors can make much more money than school counselors, in addition to being able to set their own hours. They can also become substance-abuse counselors, tutors, run educational centers and programs, or become educational or career advisors to adults.

School Nurse

School nurses do more than just hand out Band-Aids. Public health is a much-underestimated field, and living as we do in a world without epidemics and widespread disease, we often do not realize just how important it is to have a trained observer in settings such as schools. School nurses, working as they do at public facilities that are a main site for transmission of diseases and parasites, are our first line of defense against bad public health problems becoming worse. For instance, in the 2008–2009 swine flu pandemic, it was often school nurses who recognized the symptoms of the disease, alerted authorities, and had schools closed. Similarly, the school nurse's traditional monitoring of students for head lice is another aspect of this public-health function.

The school nurse is also essential in a number of quotidian functions besides first aid and comforting sick or injured children until their parents can pick them up (or, in extreme cases, until the ambulance arrives). She—99 percent of school nurses are women—helps to keep health statistics such as height and weight, participates in studies (for instance, the number of students with certain health problems), promotes healthy lifestyle and eating habits, leads anti-drug education efforts, and explains to pre-teens and teenagers the changes their bodies are going through. They help to fight preventable health problems such as childhood obesity and, in some progressive school districts, give out condoms or other birth control. In some circumstances, the nurse might recognize and report symptoms of child abuse.

The modern educational environment has added to school nurses' responsibilities. It is the nurse who dispenses ADD medication to children. It is the nurse who keeps emergency treatment available for everything from diabetic shock to anaphylaxis. If some child has a severe allergy, the nurse will work with teachers and other administrators to try to eliminate hazardous situations. The nurse might find herself giving young children with Type I diabetes insulin injections.

School nurses generally have a bachelor's degree in nursing and become registered nurses, which means passing the NCLEX-RN test. In most states, one must also pass a school-nursing certification exam. Even for those states that do not require it, the National Association of School Nurses recommends that all nurses take the National Board for Certification of School Nurses' (NBCSN) test. The position is expected to grow by 25 percent in the next 10 years due to retirements, the increased number of school-age children, and the use of schools to combat public health problems such as childhood obesity. Advancement is usually difficult (there is usually only one nurse per school), though salary increases with experience and one can become a supervisor or transfer to other careers in public health. Education is the key in this case; undergraduate and graduate degrees in public health and public health management look very impressive to employers.

Special Education Teacher

Teaching special education is easily one of the hardest jobs in the school system. By law, all students have the right to an appropriate education. It is the job of the special education teacher to deal with students who have a range of learning, emotional, and physical disabilities, ranging from the mild to the severely challenging; to come up with individual learning plans; and to serve children with disabilities to the best of their abilities. This might mean anything from a little extra help with reading to providing vocational training, teaching them how to get along in society, or simply taking care of students with profound disabilities until they "graduate" from the system or are placed in private care.

Special education teachers must be specially licensed. In addition to normal licensing and certification, they must have training in special education. The job also requires a great deal of patience, creativity, and humor. Finally, the special education teacher must have a real sense of mission—the enthusiasm to really try to motivate and help his or her students.

There is a great deal of paperwork involved in the special education process. Special education teachers often have to work even more closely with principals and other administrators to make sure that all laws, rules, and regulations are being complied with, as well as to deal with "problem" students. They must create and follow an Individual Education Program (IEP) for each student, consulting and taking input from parents, other teachers, and administrators.

There is not much room for promotion within this field, but the high degree of burnout means that many special education teachers go on to different, and often related, jobs. Special education teachers may become regular classroom teachers, or go to work for private hospitals and other institutions. They may also become tutors for children too ill to go to school. They may also become supervisors and administrators, teach special education at the college level to aspiring educators, and become mentors to junior special education teachers in exchange for a lighter teaching load.

Substitute Teacher

The "sub" is in an unenviable position. His or her job is to fill in for regular teachers, often dealing with students who see the absence as a vacation from regular work. The job can range from babysitting for a period or an hour to taking over a class for the rest of the semester. The pay can be low, the students can be insubordinate, and the lack of long-term commitment to any one school or class can mean it is hard to develop meaningful relationships with colleagues.

Substitute teachers in many districts are filled in from a pool and often paid on an hourly or per diem basis. You may spend hours or days waiting by the phone for a phone call. Other times, you may be awoken in the morning and told you are needed immediately. This can make planning, as well as financial security, difficult to achieve.

Problem Solving

Teaching Adults

Education is not only for the young: Many adults of all stages of life go back to school for a variety of reasons, ranging from furthering their knowledge and enriching their lives to advancing their certification in some field to switching careers.

Teaching adults can be very rewarding. Generally, they are more mature and disciplined. They also bring more life experience to the table. However, they are also more set in their ways. Approaches that work with younger learners might not work with adults. It is also a huge mistake to condescend to an adult learner or treat them like a child; instead, appreciate the courage it takes to admit you do not know something—and to start anew in a different field.

On the other hand, there is also a lot of job flexibility and the ability to "try on" different hats and positions in the educational system. In many places, subs are not unionized; in others, they are part of the local teacher's union.

On the plus side, there often is little bar to entry. In Alabama, for instance, you need only a high school diploma, a negative tuberculosis test, and a $10 certificate from the state. Other states and school systems require full licensure (and also pay commensurately more). Most have looser strictures for short-term subs. Also, those areas with higher educational requirements often allow you to substitute teach for a certain amount of time while working to fulfill requirements.

Substitute teachers can advance, if there is demand and they have sufficient qualifications, to become regular teachers. In such cases, the time spent as a sub can look very good on a résumé. Accordingly, investing in one's education is a very good way to spend time spent subbing.

Postsecondary Education (Two- and Four-year Institutions)

The postsecondary level is often a definitive time in a student's life. It is when he or she will make decisions that will impact the rest of their professional career, and will look to administrators, teachers, and other experienced mentor figures for counsel.

Academic Administrator

Whereas K–12 administrators usually choose a specific career path, college and university administrators might come from a diverse array of professional backgrounds. They fall into several categories: *deans, provosts,* and *chief academic officers.* The two latter categories are often interchangeable, and are in charge of administering the school. A dean is generally a professor who has become a full- or part-time administrator and is in charge of a specific program, such as a School of Arts and Sciences within a university. Deans may or may not still have classroom duties. *Directors of development* are in charge of fundraising and soliciting donations, though this is increasingly a job that falls on all members of a faculty. *Department chairs* are generally chosen from among all the professors in a department, often on a rotating basis. Being a department chair is not a popular job; you have to make all the decisions and do a lot of extra work, often for very little or no extra pay or reduction in teaching load. In addition, there are positions in charge of all aspects student life (variably called *vice presidents of student affairs* or *student life, deans of students,* and *directors of student services*) who are in charge of admissions, students' health and well-being, academic and career counseling services, international services, financial aid, housing and residential life, and social and recreational programs. *Athletic directors* oversee all aspects of a sports program—its athletes, its coaches, its finances, and its NCAA compliance. There are also administrative positions for public relations and publicity, distance learning, and information technology. *University presidents* are generally very well regarded and accomplished; they represent the top level of advancement of an academic administrator and are compensated on the level of top executives. Generally, they have years of experience as a dean or other administrator.

As you can see, there are many jobs in many capacities of university administration. All aspects of the financial, academic, and social life of the university are supervised by someone. Academic administrators do not, however, usually make hiring or tenure decisions; these are up to the individual faculties. Depending on their position, academic administrators might be hired with only a BA, or they might be academics in their own right; many PhDs who feel that they are not a good fit in the classroom, or who cannot find faculty jobs, wind up in administration. There are no certifications in this field (through formal degrees and courses of study). Generally, a doctorate in some subject is preferred for the highest levels, as it is felt that only such a person can understand all aspects of college or university life.

Administrative Staff

The smooth operation of a college or university requires a lot of organization and help. Though structures vary between schools, there are a lot of commonalities. *Registrars* are the record-keepers. They are in charge of student registration, grades, and transcripts. Obviously, this requires familiarity with database software. When alumni need transcripts, it is the registrar's office that is contacted. This is increasingly being done online, and so it is good to be familiar with these systems as well—though there is also a great deal of digging through paper, since the records of those who graduated a long time ago might not be digitized. Registrars also oversee the course catalog, the published description of all the courses offered by the university. This can mean a lot of complicated scheduling and keeping course codes straight, as well as maintaining databases. It is a good idea to be familiar with word-processing and publishing software.

Bursars (from the Latin for "purse") are in charge of students' finances. Like the registrar's job, this is being increasingly automated. Bursars need to keep track of student status, fees and other monies owed, dispensing student loans, and the procedures and checklists for various procedures. While in smaller schools this can be accomplished with little more than a phone call, in a large university, this can be quite complicated and require a great deal of paperwork. For instance, a student may not be able to register for classes before paying fees, but needs student loans to do so—however, he or she might not be able to receive the student loans before registering for classes. One must know that the correct procedure is to have the department chair or dean fill out a form assuring that the student has full-time status.

Financial aid officers work closely with admissions directors to give the necessary help to needy or worthy students. They have to both apply a school's own internal procedures and make hard decisions about who will and who will not get money (and thus be able to attend), based not only on students' merits, but on available monies and the school's need for diversity. They also need to be aware about external awards, grants, and scholarships that students can apply for.

Counselors, particularly in large schools, help students make decisions about majors and careers. They also, most importantly, make sure that they have sufficient credits in sufficient fields so that they are on track to graduate. (In many schools, this is only for under-classmen; those with majors tend to have a departmental advisor who is a professor in their field.) *Study abroad officers* help connect students with opportunities overseas, as well as prestigious fellowships such as the Fulbright and Gates Cambridge awards.

College and universities also need clerical help. There are no shortage of secretaries, receptionists, human resources directors, accountants, and other such positions.

Educational requirements vary. In some small colleges, deans and other PhD-holding staff may fulfill some of these jobs. Some administrative positions require only an associate's or bachelor's degree. (Also, some undergraduate, master's, or PhD students take jobs at their schools to receive reduced tuition while pursing a degree.)

Opportunities for advancement are the same as at any other workplace. If you are at a small school, you may need to move to another, larger institution to find a way up. In other cases, you may be promoted up the ladder to supervisor and, ultimately, director. Finally, as with much in academia, a lot hinges on education: Those with advanced degrees are looked upon more as colleagues than as employees, and are more likely to be promoted through the ranks, perhaps ultimately winding up as a top-level administrator.

Librarian

One of the fastest-growing fields in higher education, and one in which no small number of frustrated academics have found a happy home, library science is integral to the functioning of any institution of higher education. Academia depends on research, and the flow of information for scholars and researchers, whether in the form of journal articles, books, or online resources, is the librarian's stock in trade. Librarians are, as economist Olivia Crosby said, "information experts in an information age."

For a lover of knowledge, a library is heaven itself. The librarian's job is a great deal more than checking library cards, re-shelving books, and managing circulation: He or she might network globally to obtain rare books from interlibrary loan, manage the library's own collections and journal subscriptions, order books, place books on reserve for courses, make sure that fair-use guidelines are not violated, and negotiate relationships with electronic resource providers. Book preservation and re-binding are also part of the job, as are strategic planning and facilities management. Some librarians, such as those who deal with special collections, have a great deal of overlap with archivists. Their job includes cataloging, preserving, and managing access to rare books, personal papers, and other items. They tend to work for larger institutions, as well as for government agencies. Many are also active in such efforts as anti-censorship campaigns and literacy outreach.

Library subspecialties include *technical services librarians*, who handle electronic resources and subscriptions; *reference* or *research librarians*, who help patrons find works of interest to them; *collections developers*, who handle budgets and vet and acquire new books and technical resources; *systems administrators*, who update electronic card catalogs and other databases; *archivists*, who handle special collections; and *instruction librarians*, who train others to use library resources. In a smaller library, one person might handle many of these jobs; in a larger university library, each function may be filled by a large team led by managers.

College and university librarians must work closely with all parts of their institutions. They must propose budgets to the administration, as well as account for how funds are dispensed. They must administer the distribution and collection of books to students, show new students how to use the library, deal with professors' course needs, place books on reserve, request books from interlibrary loan, and perform all the other tasks needed to fill an institution's knowledge needs. To be able to guide researchers in many fields to the individual resources they need is no easy task, and one that requires a thorough knowledge of how information is organized. In addition, the job often requires working nights and weekends.

Working as a postsecondary librarian usually requires a master's of library science (MLS). Those who complete such courses will learn all about the practical aspects of library administration such as cataloging, reference, archiving, and database and Web design. Modern programs also include an information architecture component, expanding the MLS to MLIS. The exception is library technicians, who can have as little as an associate's degree. Library technicians deal with much of the grunt work such as re-shelving books, as well as cataloging, maintaining databases and records, and watching the circulation desk.

Advancement in a library depends on its size. You might be promoted to supervisory roles or even an administrative position (the university librarian or dean of libraries is the staff position in charge of all library departments, and chief information officers might come from librarians' ranks), or you might have to transfer institutions to take a better-paying job or one with more responsibility. If you do not have an MLS, obtaining one can be a path to promotion. You might also be able to teach undergraduate classes at your institution as an adjunct professor, particularly if you have an MA or PhD in another academic subject. Many librarians find their job gives them ample opportunity and resources to work on their own literary or scholarly projects.

Online Teacher

Technology has opened up many new opportunities in education. No longer do students need to sit in classrooms; online courses now make it possible to earn high school or college credit anywhere.

Generally, online teachers have a background similar to traditional teachers in their subjects. To teach high school equivalency, most accredited online instruction schools will want you to have certification; to teach college, you will need at least an MA or other terminal degree in your field. They are employed by private educational companies, as well as traditional colleges and universities.

The online teacher must know how to support their students. This goes not just for technical support, but also academic and social support. Since there is no face-to-face contact, it is hard to keep students engaged and motivated. Since many online students are nontraditional learners, one must also often coach them through academic and personal problems, teach the basics of academic writing, acculturate them to the online learning model, and try to model the thought processes that one wishes them to copy. Conversely, one must also discipline oneself to have assignments and readings posted and graded on time; it is easy to put things off until the last minute. Also, because one cannot fill time extemporaneously, online teaching generally requires more prep work than traditional teaching. Every bit of the course must be planned out, and all must add to the value of the whole.

Interacting with colleagues can be difficult for the online teacher. Generally, you have all the responsibilities of a "live and in person" teacher—grading, preparing lectures, thinking up assignments— with none of the collegial interaction. Rather, your bosses, like your students, are usually on the other end of a computer terminal. It is therefore important to be disciplined so that you have your work turned in on time and the whole mechanism of the online institution functions smoothly.

Opportunities for advancement are few. Online teaching is generally on a per-class basis (see *adjunct professor* in Postsecondary Education below), and thus hard to make into a career, but one can often parlay the experience into an adjunct professor position, or even use it as experience on a curriculum vitae toward a tenure-track professor position.

Postsecondary Teacher (Four-year School)

Though the customary title for a college teacher in the United States is "professor," technically this only applies to those who have been hired as full-time teachers in a particular academic department. The range of academic teaching jobs includes research scientists who spend little time in the classroom, writing instructors who give intensive hands-on help to students, historians who write books as well as teach, those who teach practical skills in fields such as nursing, and art and music instructors. We will discuss the main points of the job description here, as well as most of the major exceptions.

To begin with, becoming a college teacher usually requires a PhD or other terminal degree such as MD or JD. Though technically an MA is all that is required, such persons are rarely hired as full-time professors unless their outside experience or qualifications are considerable. (Exceptions include business and music schools.) This generally means that one will have to apply for and complete a doctoral program—not an easy undertaking, and one that necessitates a considerable investment of time and money. Anyone considering a job as a college-level teacher should consider this career path very carefully.

Secondly, the job market in academia is very tough. Graduate programs exist to produce PhDs. Though the overall number of open positions is expected to increase, the number of graduates is larger still. Competition is therefore high. Often, those from "name" schools (the Ivy League, top-tier state schools, and other prestigious programs) find themselves with a merited or unmerited competitive advantage in the job market. The system works, though, since colleges and universities not only receive tuition from the glut of students, but also cheap labor. Many of those who are not able to find tenure-track jobs make ends meet as *adjunct professors*, that is, part-time professors without job security or hope of promotion. While adjuncting can be a useful line on your curriculum vitae (CV, the academic equivalent of a résumé), it pays very little, requires a lot of time and energy (not to mention time spent commuting), and can result in a PhD winding up in "adjunct hell"—working for subsistence-level or less-than-subsistence level wages, unable to buy a house, start a family, pay off student loans, or otherwise lead an adult life. Graduate students may also gain classroom experience as teaching assistants (TAs) or teaching fellows (TFs). Whereas assistants help professors in larger classes, teaching fellows are usually responsible for their own classes.

Technology is making huge inroads into the classroom. Many schools are proud of their online learning systems that enable professors to share documents with the class, receive written work, and post grades. Classrooms may be wired so that multimedia and PowerPoint presentations can be used in lectures, or "smart boards" may replace the traditional blackboard. Schools may encourage or require professors to make use of these systems. Of course, tenured professors usually keep doing things the tried-and-true way they have been doing them for the past 30 years, while younger, more technologically savvy teachers will be frustrated by the layers of security red tape, lack of software and hardware updates, and incompatibilities.

Advancement in academia can be considered in two ways. One is to land a tenure-track job and rise through the ranks of assistant professor, associate professor, and full professor. The tenure process works like this: A new professor's work is generally reviewed after they have been on the job for a certain amount of time, usually three years. This usually involves some mix of classroom teaching, publication, and service to the school and the profession. If their work is deemed adequate and the other faculty respect them as a colleague, then they are granted status as an associate professor and tenure, which gives a certain amount of job security. Should tenure be denied, this is tantamount to being fired, though the unlucky scholar is usually given one year to find a new job. A well-regarded professor may, in time, be promoted by his peers to a full professorship, with commensurate increase in salary and status. (There are also distinguished professors, who are very well regarded scholars who hold endowed chairs.)

The other way to advance is to go into academic administration, becoming a dean or other officer of the school. Such persons may be considered to have left this job description and entered another, as their classroom duties will be reduced or even eliminated. For descriptions of these jobs, see Academic Administrator (Postsecondary), above.

This upward mobility may be at one institution, or a teacher may change institutions one or several times throughout their career (for instance, if a distinguished professorship opens up in another institution). Those who change schools may lose tenure and have to start all over in terms of seniority (if not salary), or may be granted tenure. Which course is taken depends on the scholar's reputation and status, as well as the details of the new school. Since academic couples often experience the "two-body problem" where available teaching jobs are located far away from one another, some may be willing to give up considerable perks in order to be closer to a spouse or family.

Professors are granted a large degree of independence in their operations. While much of the public portion of the job—lecturing—is tied to a particular schedule, other elements, such as writing books and articles and grading papers, require self-management and discipline. However, faculty members are also responsible to the other people in the school—the registrars who collect student grades, the department chairs who must file their syllabi, the students they must advise. They also must serve on committees that decide all the aspects of school life—standards, credits, program design, philosophies, etc. For those who manage research programs or receive grants, the requirements under which the various funds necessary for subsistence were dispersed must be satisfied. The untenured professor who neglects these duties is unlikely to receive tenure; the tenured professor is unlikely to be popular, and may even be dismissed.

Postsecondary Teacher (Two-year School)

In many ways, the job of a community college teacher is like that of a professor in a four-year school. Similar requirements for service and teaching also hold, and many enjoy a sort of tenure. However, there are also some important differences. First, more community college teachers hold MAs or other terminal degrees. However, due to the oversupply of PhDs, higher levels of qualification are usual, if not required. Secondly, the job tends to place a greater emphasis on teaching than on writing and research. They also tend to teach classes on a more basic level than those in four-year schools. Community college students may need more help with basic writing than, say, understanding the nuances of the Congress of Vienna.

Nonetheless, community colleges seem poised for an unprecedented expansion. President Obama has named them as a keystone in his plan to ensure that every American has at least two years of postsecondary education or training—and has followed up with this by earmarking billions of dollars of federal funds. Therefore, many future teaching opportunities will be in community colleges. Many of these will be in nontraditional academic subjects, such as nursing and applied technology. Community colleges also serve a key purpose in retraining workers in response to the demands of the labor market. Because of this, investigating the community college teaching market is well worth the time of anyone who has the credentials and an urge to teach.

Adult, Continuing, and Professional Education

Though not as well-known as secondary and postsecondary education, the following positions are nonetheless critical to the survival of the societal whole. They are opportunities to reach students who may be rediscovering their inner drive to acquire knowledge and thereby better themselves through education.

Adult Literacy and Remedial Education Teacher

Not everybody is able to or chooses to pursue the usual path of high school to college to the working world. This trajectory is especially difficult for recent immigrants, their children, and others with limited English proficiency. Adult literacy and remedial education teachers help such persons to overcome their educational deficiencies and lack of opportunities, giving them the basic communication and math skills needed to make their place in the world. Generally, students are 16 years old or older.

Adult literacy and remedial education teachers usually need to have at least a bachelor's degree. Public programs often require a public schoolteacher's license. For those who will teach non-Anglophones, a certificate for teaching English as a second language is also helpful. Classes might concentrate on reading or conversation skills, history, math, or any other academic subject. This training can tend to be less rigorous and may, in fact, only consist of a short course or test, and so this is a good profession for those who need to work while pursuing higher credentials.

Many adult literacy and remedial education teachers are volunteers with community groups. Those who teach this subject as a profession tend to be employed by community colleges, school districts, and adult learning centers. They may advance to regular, full-time teaching positions, or work in other capacities for adult learning centers or nonprofits. Those who show a good understanding of, and respect for, their students are the most likely to do well.

Adult Secondary Education Teacher

Adult secondary education teachers are in much the same situation. However, the courses they teach are designed to help adult learners achieve their General Educational Development (GED) degree. Thus, they tend to teach more advanced academic subjects. Like adult literacy and remedial education teachers, many adult literacy and remedial education teachers are volunteers with community groups, while those who teach this subject as a profession work for community colleges, school districts, and adult learning centers. Also like adult literacy and remedial education teachers, they may advance to regular, full-time teaching positions.

Museum Educator

Museums are not just exciting places for field trips; they are also places of learning. Museum educators are the specialists in museums who lead tour groups, lecture to students, and provide programs for learners of all ages at art, science, and history museums. It is their responsibility to explain often abstruse or complicated ideas and themes in the exhibits and to make museums special places for the next generation of patrons. In the past, museums were more warehouses of esoteric objects, with little in the way of explanation. Today, all that has changed: Museum educators work to make sure each exhibit tells a story and is easily understood by visitors. But that is not all a museum educator does: They also coordinate with the community, help raise funds, and provide the million-and-one things that help keep a museum's doors open. A museum educator is thus part teacher, part cheerleader, and part politician. They must be able to coordinate with curators and fund-raisers, create and stick to budgets, plan and carry out special events, and lecture to schoolchildren and PhDs alike. The work is often rewarding, but the hours are also often long.

There are many ways to become a museum educator. Learning theory, exhibit design, patron surveying, visitor evaluation, and fulfilling the museum's responsibilities as a public institution while also satisfying responsibilities to the charter, trustees, or benefactors are all part of the job. Many colleges, and many museums and institutions such as the Smithsonian, offer programs in the field. Other museum educators begin as art historians, curators, or other academic fields within the museum industry.

Museum educators must coordinate not only with others within the museum, but also with educators to help make their presentations relevant to curriculum requirements. They may move up to other positions within museum administrations, such as directorships, or gain seniority in their departments, or move to larger and better-endowed museums.

Self-enrichment Educator

"Self-enrichment" is a very broad term encompassing all the various skills that a person might want to learn—writing, sports, computer skills, tai chi, massage therapy, investment skills. The good thing is that to get started, you often need very little in the way of qualifications or certification. Merely having a good biography and claims of experience in the field, and perhaps some formal training, is quite enough. On the other hand, those with formal qualifications who deal in necessary or much-desired skills will tend to do much better.

Certification depends on the amount of regulation in your particular industry. For instance, massage therapy is often regulated at the state level. Some sports have national governing bodies, but membership is not necessarily required. Tai chi might have individual masters who tell their students when they are ready to teach. There is really no one who can tell you if you can or cannot teach senior citizens to use e-mail.

Many self-enrichment educators are entrepreneurs. To rent out a hotel auditorium and give investment or personal finance seminars requires only some up-front cash. Whether or not you actually know investment techniques or have made a lot of money in the marketplace is up to you—though, of course, selling snake oil is unethical as well as illegal.

Self-enrichment educators may work for adult-enrichment education companies, or they might be self-employed. To advance, they can see their client base grow, and even become "gurus" of their own particular brand. Writing books and making media appearances are two good ways to increase your public exposure. Some even start their own educational companies.

Chapter 4

Tips for Success

What are the keys to success in an academic career? No matter what sort of teaching you do, you will need to perform the same sorts of tasks: Find a job, interview for the position, prepare for class, get up there and teach, evaluate students' learning, counsel students, and reach those who are unmotivated or having a hard time. Plus, there are all the things that you need to do to get ahead in the field: Build a professional reputation, manage your time, look for promotions and ways up the ladder. This chapter will help you do all of these things in a professional and competent way, as well as give advice for getting ahead in your field.

Finding a Job

In order to teach, you first need to find a teaching job. How to do so will vary by your field, area of expertise, and even where you live. Some school districts and private schools advertise directly on their Web sites and in newspapers. With others, you apply directly to a central board of education. Some districts even actively recruit, especially in high-demand areas such as math and science. In other cases, you may be offered an open position because of personal connections. The college and university job market is significantly different, with open positions often posted to general academic sites and newspapers such as the *Chronicle of Higher Education*, discipline-centered networks such as the H-Net network for history, and discipline organizations such as the American Political Science Association.

The thing to remember in the job hunt is that you are no longer yourself: You are what the people hiring want. In other words, you must present yourself as the ideal candidate. We are not, of course, advocating that you lie or dissimulate or violate everything you believe to the very core of your being, such as concealing your religious beliefs or sexual orientation—or worse, pretending to be something you are not—to win a job at a religious college that requires its employees to adhere to the strictures of a particular faith. Such deception will always backfire and, besides, why would you want to put yourself in such a situation? However, you should never underestimate the importance of fitting in. If you are up for a job teaching English at a high school where they always say a prayer before the football game and the hiring committee invites you along to watch the Friday night home game, you had better bow your head along with everyone else.

Most job applications will require a cover letter. Crafting a cover letter is an art. You need to be able to emphasize both why you are the perfect candidate for the job and to fulfill all of their needs (even the ones they did not know they had), and why you will do this better than anyone else—while not stretching the truth. You should always address every point made in the job description, while also touching on the usual areas such as your education, special honors, previous experience, and (if requested) salary expectations. You should also eschew irrelevant information and empty sentiment. The people hiring you are not as interested in nebulous concepts of "team spirit" and the same platitudes about inspiring young minds that every wet-by-the-ears college graduate will put in; they want to know what makes you a good English teacher or lacrosse coach, such as your use of frequent written assignments or record of winning seasons. Avoid including too much personal information in a cover letter; the hiring committee of a very secular chemistry department might be leery if you quote St. Augustine's educational theory. *Never* put any possibly prejudicial information such as needing a job for your spouse or gratitude for their generous maternity leave in a cover letter. Even if it is illegal to discriminate on these grounds, you do not want to bias a hiring committee against you.

There are likewise many interview strategies. The usual requirements of dressing well and presenting a neat and professional appearance always hold. However, less often mentioned is that you should always behave conservatively and seriously. It is too easy for an attempt at humor to backfire. If invited out for a meal, try not to express any dietary preferences or restrictions too loudly (whereas celiac disease, for example, is difficult and dangerous to conceal, it is best to be a quiet vegetarian). Order something you can eat neatly (no lobster or chili dogs), and have no more than one alcoholic beverage, and then only if everyone else is partaking. Never give the hiring committee a reason to doubt you would fit in, such as wondering aloud if there are many other people of your religion or ethnic group in the community. Be agreeable: If they like something, then you like it, too. Also, as far as they are concerned, this job is the one you want until the day you retire.

The postsecondary academic job hunt is much harder than that for primary and secondary school jobs. There is a serious labor oversupply in higher education, partially because the "machine" runs by continually educating graduate students and turning out new PhDs—who, in turn, contribute to the labor oversupply. Your graduate adviser and other professors in your department can tell you more about how to land a job in academia than we could possibly fit into this chapter. However, there are a number of strategies that are not often mentioned, but which can be very useful.

First, consider delaying your dissertation defense a year or two until you have definite interest from hiring committees. Most schools will consider hiring a graduate student on the verge of defending, which is a fact that should go in your advisor's letter. PhDs have a very definite expiration date, and if you have not found a permanent position within a few years of your degree, you are not likely to. Also, this gives you a couple more years to improve your teaching CV by adjuncting, and it defers your student loans.

Be sure to change your cover letter to suit each school's needs and profiles. A Catholic school may appreciate the St. Augustine quote. A small private school known for their left-wing views probably will not appreciate it. While this may seem like a lot of work, you do not really have a lot of choice: hiring committees can smell a stale, re-used cover letter a mile away. Using one is a sure one-way ticket to the compost heap. Do something to distinguish yourself from others in your field. Whereas this is difficult for those in the hard sciences, engineering, and math, many arts and humanities committees cookie-cutter. Be sure to say what you will add to the life of the college or university.

Finally, do not rule out teaching at a private high school or community college. Not only are these career paths that can be much more rewarding than teaching at a lower-tier college (it is better to teach brilliant 16-year-olds than uncaring 18-year-olds), but these institutions provide supportive environments for displaced academics. There is a definite hierarchy of graduate institutions, and if you have not graduated from a top program, you may need to recognize that college teaching just is not in your near future. You can always try again in a few years—but gainful employment is your short-term need.

On the subject of publishing, make sure your dissertation is written as a book and can be easily revised into publishable form. Revising a dissertation to make it into a book is no fun when tenure hearings (and your future at your school) are rapidly approaching, your project is in a state where no editor would touch it, and you are stuck teaching four classes a semester. If your future retention and promotion lies within the "publish or perish" model, you should be planning for this *before* you even try to land a job.

How to Be a Good Teacher

Teaching is like no other career. At any level, it requires a mix of empathy, rhetoric, and showmanship. In a sense, it is like being on stage. You are always "on," and students, no matter what their age, are easily distracted and bored. Keeping their attention is critical. You must not only present the necessary material, but keep both the brightest and the slowest students in the room engaged. To do this, you need to teach in a disciplined, ordered, reasoned, and logical manner. Lectures should proceed from the most general to the specific, with students able to grasp the implications of the principles laid out in the beginning. When they have done this, they have truly mastered the material.

In order to teach in this manner, you must first know your subject. Joking around, telling stories, and playing games are no substitute for a deep knowledge of the subject. Nor is mindless activity or rote learning. Occasional digressions—the history of algebra, why there are so many officers running around Jane Austen novels—helps to enliven a lesson, but nothing will compensate for not knowing what you are talking about. You must have an in-depth, step-by-step knowledge of how the material at hand works, or else your students will know you for the fraud you are.

At the same time, do not be afraid to use humor. Humor can enliven a dull lecture, it humanizes you to your students, and helps

Everyone

Knows

Know the Law

It is illegal in the United States to discriminate in hiring based on age, race or ethnic group, sex and gender, disability, religion, or veteran status. It is also illegal to offer less than equal pay for equal work. All public employers or private firms that do business with the government must abide by these laws. (Note that none of this holds true for religious institutions, which, if they do not take federal money, including student loans, may hire and fire as they wish and based on their own criteria.)

The situation is murkier when it comes to LGBT issues. There is no federal legislation on this issue, and whereas the majority of states prohibit discrimination based on transsexualism or gender identity, enforcement varies wildly. Thus, the country is a patchwork of laws. Twelve states and the District of Columbia prohibit discrimination based on gender orientation or sexual orientation. Five have regulations or executive orders that are not laws but likewise prohibit state discrimination based on orientation and gender identity. Nine have laws forbidding discrimination based on sexual orientation only, while another three forbid this only for public employees.

Also be aware that much discrimination is not overt. While no one in modern society is likely to condone outright racism, sexism, or homophobia, laws can never overcome the fact that the needs of institutions and the needs of individuals often conflict. If you are a woman, dropping hints that you are glad for a generous health plan because you and your husband are trying to have a child may not lead to you being outright disqualified—which would be actionable under the law—but it may encourage the hiring committee to find other reasons for why you are not the best person for the job. Likewise, the simple fact of being a cancer survivor might make you *de facto* unemployable by anyone except by large state institutions, since you would drive up the group insurance premiums by an amount that would make it impossible for your coworkers to afford health insurance. In general, give away nothing of your personal life or medical history *until you are actually offered the job*.

break up the material. It lets your personality shine through, and makes you less of a discursive automaton. But remember: Everything in moderation. You are not there to be a comedian or to be your students' best buddy. Nor should jokes be at the expense of anyone in the class, or, worse, other teachers or administrators. Bullying the class to build yourself up or subverting the order of the school is the mark of a weak teacher. Likewise, you should leave risqué material and ethnic, religious, or political humor for your nightclub act.

Know that in the beginning, your presentation of material will not be the best. Accept that you will make mistakes, leave things out, skip steps, and not explain as best as you might. As time goes on and your mastery grows, you will be able to proceed flawlessly, as well as anticipate common mistakes and misconceptions. Do not try to cover for a mistake; if you do, you are cheating your students at best, and they might be missing out on critical material at worst. Apologize, go back, and try to fit the new piece of data into the existing model.

That's not all that makes a good teacher. At an absolute minimum, a teacher must have a good public-speaking voice. Nothing irritates learners of any age more than trying to take notes when the instructor is mumbling, speaking too softly, or going too fast. Thankfully, these are skills that can be learned. Learn to speak from your diaphragm. Breath-control exercises, yoga, Alexander Technique, and even singing lessons can help with this. Learn to pace your lectures so you do not speak too fast. If you need to, practice in front of a mirror—or just practice pronouncing difficult words, so you do not seem foolish.

At least half of all teaching is planning. Your lectures should be meticulously planned out, point-by-point—with visual aids, if necessary. This is where Powerpoint and other such software can help. *Never* lecture by reading a slide: The presentation should serve only to structure your talk for your students and serve as a memory aid and something around which students can take notes. As you get more experienced, you will learn how much material you can get through in a given class period.

Keeping classroom discipline is more of a concern in some milieus than others. A witty comeback is better than blustering and empty threats. Remember that every teenager's greatest fear is not of authority—it is of seeming ridiculous in front of their peers. (This is why veteran teachers always make a toilet seat or some ridiculous object into the bathroom pass.) Saying one quick phrase that undermines their standing in their peer group or makes them seem childish or foolish is worth a million angry, empty threats. Remember if they get you angry or provoke a reaction, they have won. (Also be aware of appropriate behavior—do not start playing "the dozens" with inner-city high school kids.)

No matter what, always remain in control—of the class, of the discussion, and of yourself. Discipline is of the essence. Personal anecdotes and discursions—let alone woe-is-me pity stories—have no place in the classroom. The lectern is not a confessional. You must keep a friendly, but professional, relationship with your students. You are their mentor, their guide, and their teacher—but not their buddy.

Unless you are teaching something like pure math or engineering, your personality—including your politics—is going to come out in your teaching. No matter how hard you try to keep your feelings inside, your attitudes, preferences, and tastes will make themselves evident in your tone of voice or the inopportune comment. (Some teachers, especially tenured professors, go out of their way to share their opinions with their classes, but they are the exception.) It is important to realize that this is all right. You cannot conceal who you are, though you should tone down some of your comments for public consumption—especially if they are extremely politically incorrect. Odds are, however, if you are a teacher who is known and liked, you are likely to be accepted for what you are, no matter how contrary the opinions of the surrounding community.

Never berate or criticize other teachers or administrators in front of students. To do so is not only unprofessional—it undercuts their authority. Rather, take up issues and concerns in private. It is important that the faculty present a united face in public.

Finally, one of the most important qualities in a teacher is humility and a willingness to say, "I don't know." If you do not know something, say so. Then come back the next day with an answer. The best teachers are also lifelong students—intellectually curious and always willing to learn.

Planning a Lesson

If you have taken a formal pedagogy class, or have a teaching certificate, the following information should be old hat to you. Nonetheless, many educators—those in adult education, or most university teachers—have little or no formal teaching training. For these educators, the following advice will be valuable.

First, always have an aim to the lesson. This should be loudly announced to the class at the beginning, both by telling them and by having it written on the blackboard or PowerPoint slide. Think of yourself as a tour guide telling everyone where you are going. The aim is the objective—an all-encompassing theme covering what you will be telling your students this lesson. Best of all is to state it as a question, which you can answer in the course of the lesson: "What is integral calculus?" "What is a plant?" "How did Napoleon change the balance of power in Europe?" "What are the 'right of way' rules in foil fencing?"

The Socratic method (see Chapter 1) can be a useful add-on to this method of teaching. Asking questions is a good way to get students involved and interested. First, find out what they already know. Taking the "what is a plant?" lesson above as an example, you can ask your students what they think a plant is. They will probably mention things like chlorophyll, photosynthesis, cell walls, stems, leaves, and roots. Second, you can then begin to dismantle their notions. Algae and ancient plants, for instance, do not necessarily have these things in common with modern plants. Third, you can begin to guide them toward the desired answer. For instance, you could point to stages in the embryonic development of plants as compared to that of animals. Fourth, in the end, you can lead them to the answer—for instance, that a plant is an organism that does not undergo a blastula stage.

After each question, be sure to wait for answers. Once you have some, you can then correct misapprehensions or lecture some more, filling in background information and principles. Do not go too fast: You know the answers, but your students do not. An uncomfortable silence can be OK—remember that it is more awkward for your students than for you. Stay quiet until someone ventures an answer. It is perfectly all right to put your students on the spot.

A key principle is to tell them what you are going to tell them, tell them, and then tell them what you just told them. First give the big picture: The aim, the organizing principle, the big question. Then, get into the meat of the matter. Facts and first principles should be well-organized, broken down step by step, and explained at the level your students are at. They should be able to tell you exactly what you just explained in their own words. Finally, summarize what you just told them.

As you may have noticed from these pages, examples are good things. They serve to exemplify processes, illustrate steps, and make

On the Cutting
Edge

Student Loan Readjustment

These days, it is impossible for many people to get through college without student loans. The problem is that teaching and other public-sector jobs do not tend to pay very well. Even if you only took out guaranteed federal loans, it is very possible to have payments that are so high that you cannot possibly make them and still have enough to keep body and soul together—while the interest keeps building up. What is more, student loan debt cannot be discharged through bankruptcy, and can be taken out of your social security. So, what is a would-be teacher to do?

Thankfully, Income-Based Repayment (IBR) went into effect on July 1, 2009. This federal program—which is *only* for federally insured student loan debt—caps how much you pay per month as a proportion of your discretionary income, which is defined as everything over 150 percent of the poverty level in the state in which you live. Loan consolidation is not required. Credits are also given for family size; if you have a larger family, you pay less.

Best of all, if you work in education or another not-for-profit sector, your loans can be forgiven after ten years of consistent repayment. If you work in another field, the maximum period of repayment is still 25 years. (This amount forgiven is still, however, considered income, and you will have to pay taxes on it.) There are also programs for forgiving the loans of teachers who have taken out Stafford, Perkins, and other Federal Family Education Loan Program (FFEL) loans and who teach hard-to-fill subjects such as math and science or in impoverished areas.

abstract information concrete. Always include plenty of examples in your lectures. If need be, walk students through the reasoning step by step.

Ask for synthesis of information. If your students know that Napoleon had instituted educational and social reforms that aided middle-class upward mobility, and that the political situation in Europe prior to his conquests had favored the traditional aristocracy, then they can reason out that young middle-class people might have supported his regime. On the other hand, if you ask them what their reactions to having a foreign power take over their country might be, then they will nuance their understanding of Napoleon's reforms with the knowledge that many people resented his having conquered their homelands—which in turn helped to spread nationalism. You can then continue to synthesize knowledge. Out of two facts—sometimes opposite, contradictory facts—a third truth emerges. This new truth can then be complicated with another idea, producing a new conclusion, and so on.

Key subjects, topics, and vocabulary should always be defined. Likewise, the questions you ask in class, especially those written on the board or given as class notes, should anticipate the test questions you will be giving your students in assessment. This will have two effects. First, the students will be able to pick out what is important in your lecture. Second, you will be extremely popular for "giving" the students the answers to the test questions. Of course, you will be doing nothing of the sort: You will be giving your students the tools to find the answers for themselves. However, they will have so internalized these facts, principles, and methods of reasoning that they will not remember having learned them! It only *seems* as if you are "giving" them the answers because the correct answer will seem so obvious. Conversely, the students who *have not* been paying attention will be utterly lost—but will be able to catch up if they put in the effort. You will also be able to definitively and conclusively show them *how* they were wrong.

Assessment Design

By "assessment design," we mean "how do you test students' knowledge?" Test design is a very thorny topic. These hints will help you in this key component of teaching.

The first question you should consider is how you will grade the assessment. For some subjects—extracting caffeine from tea, solving math problems, some history and literature exams, for example—there is a definite right or wrong answer. You either find the derivative of the equation or you do not; you either have a test tube full of crystals or you do not. You either know that Perseus was the mythical son of Danaë and Zeus, or not. Such assessments might be difficult, but it is hard to argue that they are graded unfairly.

If you are going to give an assignment that is qualitative in nature, be sure to set out the grading criteria *beforehand*. Generally, these are term papers and essays—difficult and laborious to grade, but not only sanctioned by tradition, they are also essential to seeing if your students have a real understanding of the subject. Having pre-defined standards makes your assessment as quantifiable and objective as possible, and therefore as much like the hard sciences and mathematics—and therefore immune to criticism—as you can make it. A good essay will outline Lincoln's rhetorical points in the Lincoln-Douglas debates, or it will not. A term paper will show how courts create *de facto* policy in the American political system, touching on issues of separation of powers and the Supreme Court cases you discussed in class, or it will not. Be sure to also specify requirements for style (papers must be grammatically correct and use proper spelling and punctuation), references (Chicago or Modern Language Association), and format (double-spaced, 12-point font, 1-inch margins, or, as an alternative that has grown more popular as online work has become more common, a given word count). Students will thus know exactly what is expected of them, and, if they receive a low grade, will have little cause for complaint.

Designing the actual questions is another issue. One approach is to simply ask students to reiterate facts and solve problems. Another is to try the synthetic approach. Multiple-choice tests can be one answer, but they limit students' creativity and, being easy to guess, do little to test real knowledge. Short-answer tests are better, perhaps with one or two essays thrown in. Another solution is take-home tests and essays. However, be careful not to write "trick" questions that exploit students' relative newness at the subject (though these might make fun extra-credit problems). No matter what solution you choose, though, make sure to mark and return the tests, quizzes, or papers in a timely fashion (not forgetting to write them down for your records!).

Athletic Coaching

Coaching a sport can be one of the most rewarding jobs in education. It is also one of the most challenging. You are given a great deal of control, both physical and psychological, over your players. It is your responsibility to do the right thing with this, and to make sure that sports become a positive experience for your team members. Remember: very, very few, if any, of your players will ever become professional athletes, and that playing sports should be a healthy experience that will set them up for a lifetime of healthy physical activity.

Giving physical punishment (laps or push-ups) as a punitive measure can be effective if athletes misbehave or slack off, but it is self-defeating if they try their best. If athletes try their hardest and the result is still not what you want, then sometimes all you can do is console them. Likewise, remember that while criticism can be constructive, praise is also necessary lest they lose heart.

Be careful with your anger level. Coaching can be very stressful, but do not let your ego dictate what you do. Nor should you let your ego get too caught up in the game. As much as it may seem the contrary, your team's win/loss ratio is not who you are as a person. Above all, do not become a tyrant and terrorize your team to think that losing makes them worthless as people—a mistaken belief which can actually make them worse, and bespeaks poor coaching more than poor playing.

Be equally careful with both the players of great ability and those of little. Schools can be extremely Darwinian environments, and social status, especially for boys, is often tied to athletic ability. However, the person who deserves the praise is not the arrogant star athlete to whom everything comes naturally and who can smoke cigarettes, miss practice, and drink beer while still leading the team in point scoring: It is the bench-sitter who tries 110 percent every practice. The former may win games, but the latter tends to win at life.

Coaching boys and girls requires very different styles. Boys, it is often said, have three things in mind—"who's got the whistle, how do I get the whistle, and how do I keep the whistle?" They fit neatly into hierarchies, and accordingly will usually do what you tell them to do without question. Girls tend to prefer discussion and consensus. Though they have their own hierarchies and status ladder, they also tend to prefer talking things out and social maneuvering to pure do-what-I-say-because-I'm-the-coach.

Likewise, dealing with problem athletes can be difficult. Benching that star athlete for misbehavior or insubordination may lose you games, but it may be necessary for the health of the team. There's a real catch-22 in this: Your job (and what people think of you) depends on your players winning, but at the same time, such an individual, especially one in a natural leadership position because of his or her athletic ability, can be detrimental to team discipline and, ultimately, performance. At the same time, coaches are increasingly being asked to set a moral and responsible tone for their team; in cases of serious misbehavior, "boys will be boys" is no longer an excuse, and you may be asked to resign for your players' action. Things like bullying, hazing, drug and alcohol offenses, and sexually or racially charged behavior are especially difficult subjects, but ones that must be nipped in the bud for the good of the athletes, the team, and the school. Perhaps the best thing you can do is to sit down with the problem athlete and explain matters in a reasoned and mature way, but always make sure that they know that being suspended or being cut from the team is a possibility. The more money, prestige, or jobs on the line, the harder the decision can be; but in the end, remember: Nobody is irreplaceable. Ask yourself what you would do if that same athlete was injured or academically ineligible, and remind yourself that their misbehavior has put you in a similarly untenable situation.

Other sorts of problem athletes are the ones who *could* be stars. Oftentimes, the biggest hurdles to this are psychological—as a professional baseball player in a slump could tell you. In such cases, sports psychology, as well as being an understanding ear or shoulder to cry on, can be essential. No matter whether it is the phenomenally talented but underweight épée fencer who throws up halfway through practice because they have not eaten all day, or the basketball player who gets intimidated when they are being guarded too closely, you need to identify and work through these problems step-by-step. *Work* is the key concept here: There are no easy fixes, and merely yelling or "motivating" is not going to cut the mustard. Rather, think outside the box. You may need to make the fencer keep a food diary so that you know they are consuming sufficient calories, or use progressive deconditioning to help your basketball player. No matter what the problem is, you need to address it creatively, progressively, and compassionately.

Remember that the most important person on the field, court, wrestling mat, or fencing piste is not the coaches, the referee, or the fans: It is the players. Everything is there for their benefit. Remember that *you* are there for *their* benefit, not the other way around. Also remember that, just as with music or art, we tend to mistakenly conflate athletic performance with a person's innermost self. Just because someone makes a bad play or has a bad habit, it does not make them a bad *person*. *Never* grade on results; grade on effort and improvement.

In the same way, movement habits that young people develop become ingrained for life. No matter what the sport, good technique is good technique firstly because it works, secondly because it is a healthy way to move. Someone with exceptional athleticism may get good results with bad movement habits—but they will not be able to rise to the top levels of the sport, and they may, in time, injure themselves badly. Likewise, good technique can compensate for mediocre ability. Therefore, you should always encourage your athletes toward good technique, as well as performance.

Finally, recognize your own limits. It may be that a certain player has a greater knowledge of the sport than you do—at least in some areas. Almost certainly, they will have greater ability, especially if they are much younger. Never penalize a player or see them as "uppity" for their skill. Instead, make use of them to train and teach new athletes—even make them an assistant coach, if they have the talent and inclination. Your job is not to prove yourself the "alpha" of the team—it is to help your players become good athletes, good teammates, and good people.

Watch Your Rep

All teachers should be extraordinarily careful with the Web and social media sites. Though these sorts of communication and networking tools have become second nature to people in their 20s and 30s, the norms that held true when you were a student still hold. To begin with, never post anything online that you do not want your students to see. Remember that your *intent* has nothing to do with it: Even if there is no desire to do harm or be a bad role model, someone can still take this information and use it against you. Also remember that the erosion of the boundary between personal and professional life does not mean that you can be more informal at work—it means that no matter what you do, you always have to keep one eye on the norms of the workplace. Pictures of you in a bikini while on vacation or enjoying a beer with friends are extremely inappropriate, and if they are online, then your students will be able to find them—much to your embarrassment.

Social media sites are an especially bad idea for a number of reasons. To begin with, you will be deluged with friend requests from students. Secondly, you do not want your students to know about your personal issues. You do not need teenagers asking you about your cat's illness or your car problems in the hallways. Likewise, you cannot control what other people send you—including material that is highly inappropriate. Even if done with the best of intentions, such over-sharing tends to erode the line between "teacher" and "friend" and diminish your authority. You are not there to be your students' buddy; you are there to be their teacher. At worst, such extracurricular contact can open you up to accusations of impropriety. The mere fact of a 35-year-old man having 15-year-old female "friends" on Facebook can be enough grounds for dismissal. If you must participate because such sites is how your family and friends participate, then be sure to set your privacy settings to the highest level and make it clear that you refuse to honor friend requests from students.

Similarly, if you have enemies or people looking for a reason to dismiss you "for cause," your Internet activity can become a very big issue very quickly. Needless to say, posting your true feelings about your incompetent bosses, hard-to-get-along-with coworkers, or even local or national politics on your blog or on message boards is a *very* bad idea. Even if you think you are anonymous, you are probably not as hard to identify as you think. This goes double if there is even a shade of violence to your words—in the post-Columbine world, such matters are never taken as jokes. The address of the originating computer can be subpoenaed, and remember that if that much effort is put into finding out an identity, then the investigators are going to want something to show for it—a firing at best, a criminal indictment at worst.

Even e-mail can be fraught with danger. Remember that typing something and hitting the "send" button can equally mean that your message disappears into the ether—or becomes a permanent record somewhere. "Friends" often stab you in the back and forward things you have written to harm you. Group e-mails and cc'ing or bcc'ing people can also come back to haunt you. What if you accidentally send that sarcastic comment about the principal's or dean's e-mail to the whole group, rather than to your one confidante? In the same way, the apparent online democracy can often lull one into a false sense of security. One adjunct professor responded to a faculty discussion list message about beautifying the campus with a criticism of the college president's revenue-raising scheme of festooning the student union with electronic billboards. Needless to say, she was not asked back to teach the following semester.

Does this mean that you need to completely abstain from electronic communications, save for the most businesslike functions? No, it does not—but you need to be circumspect. Firstly, if you are going to be a teacher, you are going to need to do some damage control. Any such pictures, blogs, or other online evidence needs to

INTERVIEW

High School Librarian

Sharon Mondschein
Library teacher (retired), Midwood High School, Brooklyn, New York

How long have you been a school librarian?
I worked as a school librarian for 28 years.

What certification and credentials do you need?
A BA/BS in any subject, a master of library science degree from an American Library Association-accredited school, and whatever local certification is required. In New York City, this means a license from the NYC Department of Education, for which one needs to pass tests in general education theory and specific subject area knowledge.

What does the job entail?
This job encompasses a spectrum of tasks. One must be familiar with the curricula of each subject area, because you must collaborate with teachers to create guidelines for lessons in all subjects. One must be knowledgeable with online search methods, databases, various specialty Web sites, and other sources of online information, as well as your own library collection. You need to be a good communicator to engage the students' attention and make sure the information you present is understood. You should know and explain the drawbacks of using only online research, and how to evaluate Web sites for accuracy and bias. You must constantly be an advocate for reading—showing how reading is both useful in everyday life, and an enjoyable pastime. A friendly attitude, good interpersonal skills, and genuinely liking kids and interacting well with them are crucial.

A school librarian must also be a good administrator. It is the librarian's job to be familiar with all levels of children's and young adult literature. This involves reading reviews of newly published books, as well as most of the books you order. You must know your budget, the tastes of both the students and staff, the needs of the curriculum, any special research needs of the staff, and be able to balance all these factors. It is also desirable to know sources for grants, and to be able to write grant proposals to help with budget shortfalls. In many schools, the librarian becomes the go-to source for grant writing across the curriculum.

How do you add to students' education?
A librarian takes students out of their classroom and into the world of information. It is the librarian who teaches research skills, how and

where to find the required information, and how to evaluate it. Often, classrooms lessons just touch on various subjects that can pique a student's interest. The librarian can direct students to more information and a deeper understanding of such subjects. The librarian's love of literature can open up the world of reading for enjoyment to students to whom reading had previously been a plodding task. Often, just the personal attention given to a student can help that student to better focus on their task.

What are the ups and downs?

For me, the high point of being a school librarian was always the personal interaction with the students. I helped kids who had never achieved scholastic success realize that they could find information on any subject and at any level easily. I found it gratifying when students who had never voluntarily walked into a library discovered that it was a fun and interesting place to be. The collaboration with my colleagues was rewarding, since it helped us both to push our boundaries and learn to work together—not an easy task for people who approached a problem from completely opposite perspectives.

The negatives include huge amounts of paperwork and all the arcane details that are go into the daily running of a library. In a large school with several librarians, the paperwork was divided up, which made it much easier to meet deadlines, and the details were shared among the librarians. However, in a small school with only one librarian, there is no one else to share the burden with, and it becomes overwhelming. Another negative is working with people who might not share your ideas and philosophies, and who are unwilling to try different methods. On the other hand, a school administration who only wants things done "their way" can be extremely debilitating to creative processes.

What room is there for advancement?

In a school system, the only advancement for librarians leads them away from direct contact with students. This advancement takes the form of moving up to working in district offices or the central office of library services. Another avenue for advancement is to become an assistant principal or principal.

What is your advice to anyone wanting to become a school librarian?

Go for it! If you love working with kids, have good people skills, are detail-oriented, and enjoy research and literature, this is the job for you. I always looked at it as the best combination of what the school system has to offer and not being locked into the usual fixed schedule that teaching usually requires.

be cleaned up. This includes anything from college or your professional life that suggests that you ever did anything illegal, morally suspect, or remotely sexual. This may involve deleting a lot of information, hiding other information, and may take some effort and e-mails to site owners or even lawyers' letters. Be sure to go deeper than just what a normal Google search brings up for you: Also follow links from friends' Web sites and personal pages, and use the site search features on any message boards or social sites. Secondly, you need to make sure any online aliases *cannot* be traced back to you. If there are details of your life that you would like to remain private, you need to bury them under a couple of layers of secondary e-mail addresses and screen names. Remember that "reasonable doubt" does not come into play here: If someone wants to use this information against you, they *will* dig, and they *will* embarrass you.

Finally, use common sense. Do not do anything that will get you in trouble, at least until you have tenure. This goes for being vociferously liberal in a highly Republican state or district (or the reverse), complaining loudly about working conditions online, or being public about your adult-oriented activities. As the Japanese expression goes, the nail that sticks up gets pounded down.

"Problem" Students

Some teachers will tell you that there is no such thing as a "problem" student—only students with problems, or students who have not yet been reached. Most educators, however, know better. The problem student can be seen to fall into one of four categories, determined by the intersections of intelligence (which we will define in the educational context as "the talent for learning and an aptitude for doing well") and the motivation to learn. In one corner is the bright student who is unmotivated or undisciplined—the underachiever. The polar opposite is the hard worker who just does not get it. Then there is the hard-working student with lots of talent—the overachiever. Finally, we have the student who is neither bright nor motivated. To deal with each category is its own skill and requires its own techniques.

The bright, unmotivated student might have one of a variety of issues. He or she might simply not be challenged. They might be more interested in their own projects, be unable to see the relevance of school to later life, or they might be *too* smart for school, recognizing the bureaucratic rigamarole for what it is. Conversely, some very intelligent people suffer from perfectionism—inability to start any project for fear they cannot make it absolutely *perfect*—ADD, or another psychological block. Some may be considered to have autism-spectrum disorders, while others may simply lack discipline or have poor work habits. Learners to whom many subjects come naturally may be unwilling to work at the difficult ones. In many cases, an educational counselor or support specialist can be of use in reaching these students. In others, all the underachiever requires is motivation, or a structure of rewards and penalties tied to performance. In time, they will hopefully build the necessary habits for a fulfilling work and academic life.

At first glance, it seems like there is nothing wrong with the overachiever. Many of these students manage it all—sports, terrific grades, extracurricular activities, volunteer work. However, few see the negative side—crippling fear of failure, abject depression when they receive one B instead of an A. Likewise, the student who is so obsessed with filling every moment of class time with his or her own insights and neurotically needing to demonstrate his or her brilliance can be more a burden—and a bore—than a pleasure. Such students are also at risk of burnout, transforming into unmotivated but intelligent students. Just as the intelligent slacker needs to be encouraged to be more active, sometimes the overachiever needs to take it easy. Likewise, sometimes overambitious parents need to stop pushing their children and let kids be kids.

Students who are motivated but do not have much talent are less frustrating, but still require patience. They will work hard, but sometimes do not seem to "get it" as quickly as other students. The trick is to support them so that they keep their motivation and drive and do not become frustrated, discouraged, or distracted. Often, the trick is finding just the right way to explain something so it "clicks." Though they should be modest with their goals, with perseverance, all things are possible.

It might seem that students who are neither bright nor motivated have no place in school. They can be troublemakers, cutting class, not doing work, or being disruptive. The downside is first, that they will eventually need to find a place in society, which in turn depends on their being socialized in school, and second, as much as they may fail the educational system, it is important that the educational system not fail them. Such students need a great deal of encouragement and support. Sadly, if their outside environment does not support academic achievement, they are unlikely to see school as important. Nonetheless, if they do drop out, they should also be made aware of adult-education, GED, community college, and other such programs.

Having been raised in a society obsessed with self-esteem, winning for everyone, and "everyone is special," students often become flustered when they hit the brick wall of a teacher who demands accountability. Surely, they think, they deserve a break? Surely, their case is exceptional, their story so moving, their needs so pressing, that they deserve an extension or an increase in their grade? Just as we are more likely to point out the splinter in our neighbor's eye than the timber in our own, many students do not see the forest for the trees, recognizing that specific actions on their part led to the situation they are in.

Problem Solving

The False Accusation

Professor K., a very junior instructor at a university known for its left-liberal leanings, was astounded. She had received a notice from her dean that a student had accused her of racial discrimination and summoning her to mediation. Such a thing had never happened to her before, and even the onus of having been accused could be career-ending. Not only could she not recall ever having said such anything that could be seen as racially insensitive, but such practices went against her own deeply-held beliefs.

Upon investigation, the reason why she could not recall any such incident became apparent. Professor K.'s accuser was a senior who needed her class to graduate. Yet, he had not once made an appearance in her classroom all semester. When he had contacted her via e-mail some weeks before the term ended seeing what he could do to pass the class, she responded, naturally, that, not having done the work, he could not receive credit. Desperate, the student had made up a false accusation of racial discrimination.

Because she had kept careful attendance records, and because the student was unable to produce any evidence that he had indeed had had any interaction with her, Professor K. was easily able to exonerate herself from the charges, and her reputation was unsullied.

Sometimes failure is what is needed for personal growth. We often learn more from our errors—whether it is that we had to study our multiplication tables or that we are not cut out to be a physician—than our successes. American society, with its every-man-for-himself-and-devil-take-the hindmost attitude, is adverse to failure. With so little social safety net, we do not like to contemplate the consequences of failure—least of all, it happening to us. What does this mean for the teacher? Be understanding—up to a point. Let it be known that there are definite, concrete expectations, and that there are definite consequences if these expectations are not met.

According to the National Institutes of Health, some one-quarter of American adults suffer from some form of mental illness in a given year. Symptoms of these diseases often emerge in childhood and the adolescent years. The teacher is often the first to notice. In case you suspect ADHD or bipolar disorder, the proper thing to do is to refer the student to counselors for proper evaluation. Do not remain silent—a student's future could rest on your actions.

Likewise, college campuses have become far more proactive about mental health issues. High-profile cases such as the Virginia Tech shootings are only part of the reason: Many schools fear being held liable for student suicides, assaults, or stalking behavior. The result, in many cases, is to exclude the students from campus—which, by eliminating their social safety net and contributing to feelings of alienation, can make some problems worse. As a result, many professors are loathe to get involved, or to try to intervene themselves. These are both mistakes. Besides the fact that this opens you up to liability, you may be keeping the student from getting the help they need. Do, however, be encouraging and supportive of your students in such circumstances, and do advocate with the deans and other administrators that they be allowed to return to campus.

Finally, classroom disruption is not to be tolerated. A student may have the right not to learn, but he or she does not have the right to interfere with others' education. When dealing with problematic students or disruptive behaviors, *never* become agitated. If you do, then the student has won—whether or not that was his or her goal. Count to 10, take deep breaths, or do whatever it is you have to do. Never lower yourself to the students' level. (Also, it is far easier to think of a witty response when you are calm.)

Cell phones are the bane of modern existence. They are ubiquitous, and one often forgets to turn it off in critical situations. We have found that the number-one way to remind students to do this is to take out our phone at the beginning of class and ostentatiously turn off the ringer (the clock can then be used to time the lecture). Do not forget your phone after class, though!

Talking in class is not only rude—it disrupts the learning process by making you lose your train of thought and distracting the other students. While some talking ("What did he just say?" "That you cannot divide by zero") is inevitable and even healthy, continued irrelevant conversations are not good. You can deal with this problem in several ways. A stony silence and pointed stare usually do the trick. If the students continue, a few reminders such as "This will be on the final," or "I think your classmates will need this information, since *they* want to pass this class, so will you please stop disturbing them?" The latter is a particularly good strategy, since it puts your overly social students in the role of the outsiders. It is best to save your harshest invective, such as threatening grade reduction, for dealing with repeat offenders outside of class.

Many students think it is OK to arrive late and leave early. If a student has a legitimate need to leave early (they have only 10 minutes to make a 15-minute drive to pick up their child), then this can be arranged, and they can sit near an exit so as to be less disruptive. However, as a general rule, it is undisciplined and disruptive. Rustling of papers, zipping of bags, and donning of outer garments are incredibly distracting. The best solution is to give important information, hand-outs, and pop quizzes at the beginning and end of class—and then do not repeat it or allow extra time. Also make it clear (if you take attendance) that late arrival is equivalent to absence.

Cutting class is a similar problem. There is not much that can be done about this—save to let it be known that non-attendance has significant penalties. Make the consequences known straight off the bat, and do not give students a break for this.

Converse to the problem of cutting class, there is a growing problem of students being *too* present. E-mail and online learning have eroded the distinction between personal and private life. Set limits. Make it clear that you will not answer e-mails after a certain hour, and that it is up to students to ask questions or hand in assignments in a timely manner. Then, stick to your rules. Many students will be resentful of this—but if you have made the boundaries clear, it is up to them to respect this. No administrator will ever require you to be "on" 24 hours a day.

Some students try to monopolize class time—whether to show their lack of respect for authority, because of some other psychological issue (in which case it is appropriate to refer them to counseling), to push a certain viewpoint (not uncommon when one covers controversial subjects such as evolution or constitutional law), or out of a neurotic need to share their insights or for some sort of affirmation. Sometimes, they want to drive the class off on an irrelevant tangent only interesting to them, or wheedle out answers or test questions. Sometimes, students ask questions you have already answered. In such cases, one can always return the class on-track by suggesting they can see you after class. In others, you can shut them down by suggesting they research the question themselves and come back with an answer for the next class. Alternately, you can put out a question box into which they can drop questions. Students can ramble on—in which case it is appropriate to ask them to cut to the chase—though more commonly, one has students who are too shy to speak up and who need to be encouraged or even called on (particularly when you know that they know the answer). Encouraging the quiet and shutting down the verbose is a huge part of classroom management.

Modern students also have no idea how to dress, thinking that proper respect to the educational environment is shown by flip-flops, pajama bottoms, and the briefest of halter tops. Commenting on such garb ("That's a lovely brassiere, Ms. Smith, but I wish you wouldn't display it in my class") is likely to get you into trouble. Nor are dress codes particularly in vogue in the modern higher educational environment. The best thing you can do is set an example by always looking neat and professional, and if possible, turn the air conditioning up to a rather chilly temperature.

Overall, classroom management comes down to a core set of principles: Set and stick to limits. Be consistent. Be sure that students take responsibility for themselves, and, conversely, make sure your material is accessible to them. Respect your students, and your students will respect you.

Upward Mobility

The question of promotion is a sticky one for primary and secondary school teachers. After all, the job is not really *per se* designed for advancement. One enters the classroom, and, provided one does a competent job, is granted tenure. Pay raises come with seniority, until, after a given period of time, one can retire with full benefits. The joys of the job come not from upward advancement, but from seeing one's students grow and develop.

This is not, however, to say that mobility is not possible. After all, half of all teachers quit within five years; not all of them leave the educational field. Below are some possibilities for moving not just upwards, but also sideways into related fields to which you might be better-suited.

The first possibility is to enter academic administration. This can be on the school, district, or state level. Possible jobs include dean, vice principal, principal, superintendent, curriculum developer, and administrative positions at the state level. For higher positions, you will usually need a combination of years of experience, higher educational qualifications (a PhD in education or a related field is often a minimum requirement), and a knowledge of the field to work your way up the ladder. Academic administrators usually have their own credentialing process, which varies by state—though in some places where there is a perceived need for academic leadership, such as New York City, there is an administrative fast track. No matter where you go, you will need to complete the training process and usually a probationary period. It also helps to know people and to be able to play the political game. This is especially true at the district and state level, where jobs can be dispensed in a sort of patronage system, and not necessarily to the most qualified applicant.

The second possibility is to change schools or systems. For instance, it is entirely possible for a disillusioned public school teacher to put his or her certification and experience to work looking for a job in a private school, perhaps one with an alternative educational philosophy. Likewise, elite private schools can provide a home for teachers wishing both higher pay and a higher quality of students. In order to make this change, you will need not only education and experience, but also sterling credentials and recommendations. You can also, and with somewhat more ease, go to a better school in the same system, or from a junior high school to a high school. Usually, however, this requires an application process and waiting for an available position—though, again, knowing someone can help.

The third possibility is to do something involving the education of educators—that is, becoming a college professor or outside consultant. Again, a PhD is a minimum requirement. Jobs in this field can be scarce. If you go into business for yourself as a consultant, networking and contacts are essential—and the higher the level, the better. Likewise, it can be hard to get your foot in the door as a college professor—but once you do, the same career advice that goes to postsecondary teachers applies to you, too.

Finally, you can enter a field outside, but related to, education. Textbook publishers, for instance, are eager for former teacher with writing and editing skills. Libraries, corporate trainers, and other employers in the government, not-for-profit, and for-profit sectors are also possibilities.

For postsecondary teachers, the path to advancement is a little clearer. Generally, there is a steady promotional path from a non-tenured assistant professor to associate professor to, later in one's career, distinguished chairs and other honors. Such tenure and promotion is usually based on a combination of research and publication, teaching, and service. "Publish or perish" is usually the name of the game, though some schools, and especially small liberal arts colleges and community colleges, place a much higher value on teaching and service than others. If you are unhappy at a job, want to be closer to a spouse, or want to take a new direction in your career, you can also apply a position at a different college or university. Be careful doing this: Shopping around for a new job can ruin your reputation in your department. It can also mean that you have to give up tenure and start anew. If your scholarly reputation allows, you can also move up to a more prestigious school.

Academics can also become academic administrators—deans, directors, even university presidents. For those who want to still be part of university life and even have the opportunity to publish and/or teach, but do not want to be burdened with everything a professor has to do, this can be an ideal career path. The job is usually year-round, but is also a lot more predictable and usually has a higher salary. In this, academic administration can represent a real step up with more responsibility, better pay, and a chance to really make a difference in the academic environment. On the other hand, it can take you out of direct contact with students, mean the end (or curtailing) of a research career, and lead to a feeling of having lost everything that made you want to become a teacher in the first place.

Chapter 5

Talk Like a Pro

As with any professional field, a working knowledge of terms, expressions, and key organizations is essential in your dialogues with others. Study the glossary below to get a head start on comprehending the educator's basic vocabulary, and consult it whenever you hear a new expression on the job.

AAC&U Association of American Colleges and Universities, a national association that is committed to improving undergraduate education and advancing liberal education as the preferred philosophy of education for all students. (Formerly known as the AAC.)

AAUP American Association of University Professors. Its stated mission is to advance academic freedom and shared governance, to define fundamental professional values and standards for higher education, and to ensure higher education's contribution to the common good.

academic freedom The belief that the freedom of inquiry by students and faculty members is essential to the mission of the academy. In the United States, academic freedom is generally taken as the notion of academic freedom defined by the "1940 Statement of Principles on Academic Freedom and Tenure," jointly authored by the American Association of University Professors (AAUP) and the Association of American

Colleges (AAC) (now the Association of American Colleges and Universities). These principles state that, "Teachers are entitled to freedom in the classroom in discussing their subject." The statement also permits institutions to impose "limitations of academic freedom because of religious or other aims," so long as they are "clearly stated in writing at the time of the appointment."

accelerated middle schools   Self-contained academic programs designed to help middle school students who are behind grade level catch up with their age peers. If these students begin high school with other students their age, the hope is that they will be more likely to stay in school and graduate. The programs serve students who are one to two years behind grade level and give them the opportunity to cover an additional year of curriculum during their one to two years in the program. Accelerated middle schools can be structured as separate schools or as schools within a traditional middle school.

achievement level   Established categories of performance that describe how well students have mastered the knowledge and skills being assessed.

ACT   A privately owned national test that many colleges and universities require as part of a student's application package. The ACT is designed to establish mastery of a generalized curriculum spelled out in the Standards for Transition or College Readiness Standards. The ACT is a multiple-choice test that now offers an optional writing test. Research conducted in conjunction with the Education Trust showed that rigorous adherence to high standards in courses taught by well qualified teachers resulted in ACT scores correlated with success in freshman college courses.

adequate yearly progress   The No Child Left Behind Act of 2001 requires that each state shall establish a timeline for achievement of that state's standards, with yearly benchmarks to be achieved along that path. (Also known as "AYP.")

alternative assessment   An assessment model in which students, teachers, and sometimes parents select pieces from a student's combined work over the (usually four) years of school to demonstrate that learning and improvement has taken place over those years. It emphasizes the learning process as an active demonstration of knowledge. Alternative assessments are used to encourage student involvement in their assessment, their interaction with other students, teachers, parents and the larger community. It is in contrast to *performance evaluation.*

alternative school   Any school that that differs from the norm, (and, as such, is difficult to describe categorically). They may cater to students with physical, mental, or emotional difficulties; unusually bright students who engage in self-directed learning; or employ unusual pedagogical techniques. One, the Harvey Milk School in New York City, was chartered to provide a safe and supportive school space for lesbian, gay, bisexual, transgender or questioning teenagers.

andragogy   Learning strategies focused on adults, (as opposed to *pedagogy*, which is technically focused on children, although it often refers to all education). Andragogy often stresses engaging adult learners with the structure of learning experience.

AP examinations   Tests owned and administered by the College Board to allow students to get credit for college-level work while in high school. Teachers attend courses offered by the College Board to familiarize themselves with the AP syllabus in 20 subject areas. The examinations consist of multiple-choice and essay questions, although a few AP examinations, such as Studio Art, require the submission of a portfolio of work. Colleges and universities will sometimes award college credit to students with a high score (three or higher) on an AP examination. However, this is no guarantee, because different institutions have different policies about accepting AP scores.

Averaged Freshman Graduation Rates (AFGR) for Public School Students   Collected by the NCES, the averaged freshman graduation rate is an estimate of the percentage of public high school students who graduate on time—that is, four years after starting ninth grade—with a regular diploma. The rate uses aggregate student enrollment data to estimate the size of an incoming freshman class and aggregate counts of the number of diplomas awarded four years later. Although not as accurate as an on-time graduation rate computed from a cohort of students using student record data, this estimate of an on-time graduation rate can be computed with currently available data. The AFGR was selected from a number of alternative estimates that can be calculated using cross-sectional data based on a technical review and analysis of a set of alternative estimates. AFGR estimates are based on the Common Core of Data, State Nonfiscal Survey of Public Elementary/Secondary Education, with ungraded enrollments distributed proportionally to reported enrollments by grade.

BA   Abbreviation for the college degree *bachelor of arts.*

back to basics   Long-established educational customs that society has traditionally deemed appropriate. Back to basics is often a conservative response to education reform initiatives.

BFA   Abbreviation for the college degree *bachelor of fine arts*, generally given to those who have graduated with a professional degree in visual or performing arts (such as from a conservatory).

Blaine Amendments   Wording added to most state constitutions in the 1870s which stipulated that no public monies could be used to fund religious schooling. Named after Senator James G. Blaine of Maine, who, like many Protestant Nativists, feared growing Catholic influence.

block scheduling   A type of academic scheduling in which each student has fewer classes per day for a longer period of time. This is intended to result in more time for teaching due to less class switching and preparation. In some programs, a block schedule means taking one class at a time, all day, every day, until all of the material is covered.

Brown v. Board of Education   1954 Supreme Court decision that overturned Plessy v. Ferguson. "Separate but equal" was recognized as inherently unequal.

BS   Abbreviation for the college degree *bachelor of science.*

BSW   Abbreviation for the college degree *bachelor of social work.*

bubble test   Students face a question with four or five possible answers and respond by filling in a blank "bubble" with a number two pencil. Why a number two pencil? Because the lead in the pencil is a conductor of electricity so that the answer sheets can be scored by machine.

charter schools   Elementary or secondary schools in the United States that receive public money but have been exempted from some of the regulations that apply to other public schools. This is usually done in exchange for accountability in producing results, which are set forth in each school's charter. While charter schools provide an alternative to other public schools, they are part of the public education system and do not charge tuition. Where space at a charter school is limited, admission is often allocated by lottery. Some charter schools provide a curriculum that specializes in a certain field—for example, arts or mathematics. Others attempt to provide a better and more efficient general education than nearby public schools.

collaborative learning   A general term for a variety of approaches that involve joint effort by students or students and teachers. Each student depends on and is accountable to the others. Groups of students work together in searching for understanding, meaning, or solutions. Closely related to *cooperative learning.*

College Board   A not-for-profit membership association founded in 1900 that serves seven million students and their parents, high schools, and colleges through programs and services in college admissions, guidance, assessment, financial aid, enrollment, and teaching and learning. Among its best known programs are the Standard Aptitude Test (SAT) and the Advanced Placement Program (AP).

Common Core of Data (CCD)   The Common Core of Data (CCD) is a program of the U.S. Department of Education's National Center for Education Statistics that annually collects fiscal and non-fiscal data about all public schools, public school districts, and state education agencies in the United States. The data are supplied by state education agency officials and include information that describes schools and school districts, including name, address, and phone number; descriptive information about students and staff, including demographics; and fiscal data, including revenues and current expenditures.

community college   Primarily two-year public institutions providing higher education and lower-level tertiary education, granting certificates, diplomas, and associate's degrees. These schools meet a need for a level of education that is more accessible and less expensive than four-year universities, but greater than high school. After graduating from a community college, some students transfer to a four-year liberal arts college or university for two to three years to complete a bachelor's degree. Also referred to as junior colleges, technical colleges, or city colleges.

compulsory education   Education that children are required by the laws of a given state to receive. It is often closely associated with public education, the education that a state provides universally to its citizens. In some places homeschooling may be a legal alternative to attending state-provided school.

computerized adaptive testing   A method for administering tests that adapts to the examinee's ability level, also called *tailored testing*. For example, if an examinee performs well on an item of intermediate difficulty, he or she will then be given a more difficult question. Or, if he or she performed poorly, the examinee would be given an easier question.

constructed response test   *See* open-ended test.

cooperative learning   An environment in which students interact in groups and mutually contribute to the learning process. (Cooperative learning is contrasted with curriculum-driven education.)

corporal punishment   A method of discipline in which a teacher or administrator inflicts pain upon the student. It usually involves methodically striking the student with an implement such as a paddle, ruler, or stick.

cram school   A specialized school that trains its students to meet particular goals, most commonly to pass the entrance examinations of high schools or universities. The English name is derived from the slang term "cramming," meaning to study hard or to study a large amount of material in a short period of time.

criterion-referenced test   A test that determines the degree to which the examinee has learned the material in question. Most tests and quizzes written by school teachers are criterion-referenced tests. Criterion-referenced assessment is contrasted with norm-referenced assessment and ipsative assessment. In contrast to norm-referenced tests, it is theoretically possible for all students to achieve the highest—or the lowest—score, because there is no attempt to compare students to each other, only to the standards. Results are reported in levels that are typically basic, proficient, and advanced. The test items are not chosen to sort students but to ascertain whether they have mastered the knowledge and skills contained in the standards. Because standards are usually far more numerous than could ever be included in a test, test designers work with teachers and content specialists to narrow down the standards to essential knowledge and skills at the grades to be tested. The number of criterion-referenced tests in use at the state level has dramatically increased since NCLB was implemented in 2001 because they measure achievement of the knowledge and skills required by state standards.

On the Cutting Edge

The SAT-Optional Movement

The SAT has long been controversial. Critics charge that it is inaccurate and favors students of privileged demographic, ethnic, income, and cultural backgrounds. They also criticize that standardized testing as a whole does not provide fair, balanced, or educationally useful evaluations. If students' scores on such tests can be improved by coaching, they charge, then they are not really an accurate gauge of learning. Moreover, they are not regulated by any independent authority. Recently, much of the criticism has been directed at the SAT, with the result of more and more schools making the test optional. The National Center for Fair and Open Testing maintains a Web site at Fairtest.org, listing (as of 2009) over 830 SAT-optional schools.

Defenders of such tests disagree, holding them up as scientifically- and statistically-proven indicators of success. Also, schools that eliminate such tests for their prospective students will tend to show higher metrics for their incoming freshmen, having eliminated the low scorers.

cura personalis   One of Ignatius Loyola's educational principles upon which he founded the Society of Jesus, or Jesuits. Literally "care of the person," but perhaps better translated as "individual attention." What this means is, firstly, that the whole person must be educated: intellectually, physically, spiritually, and morally. In many ways, this draws from the classical model proposed by the ancient Greeks and continued by the Romans.

cutscore   The pass-fail point in a test. The examinee passes if his or her score is above the cutscore and fails if it is below the cutscore. (Most criterion-referenced tests involve a cutscore.)

discovery learning   A method of *inquiry-based learning* which takes place in problem solving situations. The underlying concept of this philosophical movement is that students should "learn by doing."

distance learning   See virtual education.

EdD   Abbreviation for the college degree of doctorate offered in the field of education.

Elementary and Secondary Education Act   Enacted by congress April 11, 1965, this funds primary and secondary education, while explicitly forbidding the establishment of a national curriculum. (Also known as the "ESEA.")

elementary school   See *primary school.*

formative assessment   This assessment provides information about learning in process. It consists of the weekly quizzes, tests, and even essays given by teachers to their classes. Teachers and students use the results of formative assessments to understand how students are progressing and to make adjustments in instruction. Not all formative assessment is teacher-designed. Textbook publishers now include in their packaging CD-ROMs of tests aligned to the chapters in their books. Additionally, test publishers have begun to supply assessments for use at intervals in the classroom (frequently at every six or every nine weeks). These benchmark tests are aligned to the state standards and tests that students will take for accountability purposes.

GED   General Educational Development (or GED) tests are a group of five subject tests which, when passed, certify that the taker has American or Canadian high school-level academic skills. To pass the GED tests and earn a GED credential, test takers must score higher than 40 percent of graduating high school seniors nationwide. Some jurisdictions require that students pass additional tests, such as an English proficiency exam or civics test. The GED is sometimes referred to as a "General Equivalency Diploma" or "General Education(al) Diploma." The American Council on Education is the sole developer for the GED test. The test is always taken in person and never available online. Jurisdictions award a "Certificate of General Educational Development" or similarly titled credential to persons who meet the passing score requirements. Only individuals who have not earned a high school diploma may take the GED tests. The tests were originally created to help veterans after World War II return to civilian life.

GI Bill   Act of congress passed in 1944, one of the provisions of which was that the government would pay toward college or trade school tuition for veterans. The GI Bill was drafted to cope with the glut of labor that was precipitated by the end of World

War II. By 1965, 1.2 million veterans had gone to college on the GI Bill, over 860,000 had used it for other education, and 318,000 had sought occupational training. The result was a dramatic increase in the educated, home-owning middle class.

Graduation Really Achieves Dreams (GRAD) An initiative of the U.S. Department of Education for students in economically disadvantaged communities that aims to reduce dropping out and increase rates of college enrollment and graduation by increasing reading and math skills, improving behavior in school, and providing a service safety net. At the high school level, Project GRAD provides four-year college scholarships and summer institutes to promote attending and completing high school. Project GRAD also provides services in those elementary and middle schools that feed in to the participating high schools.

growth model A method for measuring the amount of academic progress each student makes between two points in time. For example, Otis showed a 50 point growth by improving his math score from 300 last year in the fourth grade to 350 on this year's fifth grade exam.

Head Start A federal program aimed not only at giving low-income children healthy and developmentally normal early childhoods, but also providing educational intervention. It began in 1961 under the Department of Health and Human Services, and was revised under the Head Start Act of 1981. By 2005, over 22 million children had participated. The 2005 budget also allocated $6.9 million for 905,000 children.

higher education Education that is provided by universities, vocational universities, community colleges, liberal arts colleges, institutes of technology, and other collegiate level institutions (such as vocational schools, trade schools, and career colleges) that award academic degrees or professional certifications.

High School Redirection An alternative high school program of the U.S. Department of Education for youth considered at risk of dropping out. The program emphasizes basic skills development (with a particular focus on reading skills) and offers limited extra-curricular activities. The schools operate in economically disadvantaged areas and serve students who have dropped out in the past, who are teen parents, who have poor test scores, or who are over-age for their grade. To foster a sense of community, the schools are small and teachers are encouraged to act as mentors as well as instructors. High School Redirection was found to have mixed effects on staying in school, potentially positive effects on progressing in school, and no discernible effects on completing school.

high-stakes test   A test for which the consequences for failure are grave. For instance, a student who does not pass a high-stakes test might not be promoted to the next grade or receive a diploma. A school or district that does not have a certain percentage of students pass a test might lose funding, and teachers might even be fired. State testing to document Adequate Yearly Progress (AYP) in accordance with NCLB is called "high-stakes" because of the consequences to schools (and of course to students) that fail to maintain a steady increase in achievement across the subpopulations of the schools (i.e., minority, poor, and special education students).

homeschooling   The education of children at home, typically by parents but sometimes by tutors, rather than in a formal setting of public or private school. In the modern sense, homeschooling is an alternative in developed countries to formal education. It is also an alternative for families living in isolated rural locations or living temporarily abroad.

I Have A Dream   A program that encourages students in low-income communities to complete high school and go on to college. The program guarantees that tuition for higher education will be covered after high school graduation. In addition, it provides participants with tutoring and counseling from elementary school through high school. Each I Have A Dream program sponsors either an entire grade level of students at a low-income public elementary school or an entire cohort of same-age children in a public housing development. These students are tracked over time and encouraged to participate in program activities, such as tutoring, mentoring, counseling, community service, and recreational opportunities. A full-time paid staff member coordinates program activities and serves as a mentor to program participants. A group of sponsors commits to working with the students throughout the life of the program and often provides the program with funding and other resources. The sponsors and other local donors ensure that participants who graduate from high school receive postsecondary education tuition assistance.

inquiry-based learning   A learning method in which teachers create situations in which students are to solve problems. Lessons are designed so that students make connections to previous knowledge, bring their own questions to learning, investigate their own questions and design ways to try out their ideas. Such investigations may extend over a long period of time. Students may communicate through journal writing, oral presentations, drawing, graphing, charting, etc. Students then revise their explanations as they learn. This technique is particularly popular in science instruction, but has also been used in a number of other subject matter areas including mathematics, engineering, and even reading instruction.

institute of technology   A research-intensive university with a focus on engineering, science, and technology. (Also known as a *polytechnic institute* or *polytechnic university*.)

International Baccalaureate (IB)   Like AP, which is a combined program of courses and examinations, the IB offers a course of instruction and examinations that allow U.S. students to gain credentials equivalent to those in European schools. The program begins at the grammar school level and continues through the end of high school, although students can enroll at any point. The assessments consist of essays except for problems in mathematics and science.

ipsative assessment   Assessing a pupil's present performance against his or her prior performance. (Latin for "of the self.") Contrasted with criterion-referenced assessment and norm-referenced assessment, ipsative assessment can be particularly useful for children with learning disabilities and can improve motivation. It features heavily in physical education and also in computer games. Encouraging pupils to beat their previous scores can take peer pressure out of situations and eliminates the competitive element associated with norm-based referencing.

Ivy League   An athletic conference comprising eight private institutions of higher education in the Northeastern United States. The term has connotations of academic excellence, selectivity in admissions, and social elitism. The schools of the Ivy League are: Harvard University, Yale University, the University of Pennsylvania, Princeton University, Columbia University, Cornell University, Brown University, and Dartmouth College.

Jesuits   A Roman Catholic religious order founded in 1534 by
a former Spanish soldier named Ignatius Loyola. In addition
to being one of the Roman Catholic Church's weapons in
fighting the Protestant Reformation, they were founded with
the purpose of educating young people irregardless of social
or economic status. There are hundreds of Jesuit colleges and
universities around the world—28 in the United States—as well
as many primary and secondary schools. The Jesuit order is also
known as the Society of Jesus.

Job Corps   A federally funded education and job training
program for economically disadvantaged youth, offering
remedial education, GED (General Educational Development)
preparation, vocational training, job placement assistance, and
other supports. Job Corps participants typically reside in a Job
Corps center while enrolled in the program and can remain in
the program for up to two years.

JOBSTART   An alternative education and training program
of the U.S. Department of Education designed to improve
the economic prospects of young, disadvantaged high school
dropouts by increasing educational attainment and developing
occupational skills. The program has four main components: (1)
basic academic skills instruction with a focus on GED (General
Educational Development) preparation, (2) occupational
skills training, (3) training-related support services (such as
transportation assistance and childcare), and (4) job placement
assistance. Participants receive at least 200 hours of basic
education and 500 hours of occupational training.

K–12   Shorthand for the years including kindergarten through
12th grade, the first and last grades of free education in the
United States, Australia, and English Canada.

learning management system   Software for delivering,
tracking, and managing education or training programs,
ranging from systems for managing records to software for
distributing courses over the Internet and offering features for
online collaboration.

liberal arts   Curriculum that imparts general knowledge
and develops the student's rational thought and intellectual
capabilities, unlike the professional, vocational, technical
curricula emphasizing specialization. The contemporary liberal
arts comprise art, literature, languages, philosophy, politics,
history, mathematics, and science.

low-stakes testing   Low-stakes testing has no consequences outside the school, although the results may have classroom consequences such as contributing to students' grades. Formative assessment is a good example of low-stakes testing.

MA   Abbreviation for the college degree *master of arts*, the first level of postgraduate study in arts after the bachelor's degree.

madrassa   A Muslim school, college, or university that is often part of a mosque.

magnet school   Public schools with specialized courses or curricula. "Magnet" refers to how the schools draw students from across the normal boundaries defined by authorities (usually school boards) as school zones that feed into certain schools. There are magnet schools at the elementary school, middle school, and high school levels. Some magnet schools are established by school districts and draw only from the district, while others (such as Maine School of Science and Mathematics and Commonwealth Governor's Schools in Virginia) are set up by state governments and may draw from multiple districts.

matrix test   A test that is divided among students, so that two students sitting next to each other may not be looking at the same question.

MBA   Abbreviation for the college degree *master of business administration*, for those who study scientific approaches to management of business and industry.

MFA   Abbreviation for the college degree *master of fine arts*, awarded for graduate education in the arts such as dance, writing, and sculpture.

middle college high school   Alternative high schools located on college campuses that aim to help at-risk students complete high school and encourage them to attend college. The schools offer a project-centered, interdisciplinary curriculum, with an emphasis on team teaching, individualized attention, and development of critical thinking skills. Students are also offered support services, including specialized counseling, peer support, and career experience opportunities.

mini-mester   A portion of the school year in which students take one course taught at an accelerated pace, usually over three or four weeks, instead of a full academic quarter or semester.

Montessori method   An alternative education system. Billing itself as "child-centered," the Montessori method has teachers,

Professional
Ethics

The Bennington Tenure Case

Bennington College in Vermont has long been held up as a bastion both of privilege and of unconventional thought. Notable alumni include artists, writers, and actors such as Brett Easton Ellis, Donna Tartt, Kiran Desai, and Alan Arkin. The curriculum was free-flowing, with students given written evaluations rather than grades. Rather than a formal tenure system, professors were given two- and three-year contracts, with "presumptive tenure" at the five-year mark.

In 1994, this radically changed when the school's Board of Directors initiated a massive reorganization. Twenty-seven professors, of which two-thirds had presumptive tenure, were told their contracts would not be renewed. This represented almost half the teaching faculty, and was the end of two years of political struggle between the faculty, who saw themselves as ultimately responsible for the school, and the increasingly autocratic board. Teachers in dance, art, and music would not be academics, but "practicing" artists and professionals. Seventeen of the professors sued, and the school was censured by the American Association of University Professors. The professors' lawsuit was settled in 2000 for almost $1.9 million and an apology from the college.

The Bennington case does not end happily—some of the professors found other jobs, while others retired from academia—but it does illustrate an important point. The school *did* have severe financial problems at the time of the restructuring. However, academic freedom, and the tenure system, are more valuable to some than gold.

known as "directors," not teaching in the formal sense, but rather presenting carefully chosen and constructed materials that engage all five senses and allow children to explore their world and derive concepts and abstract principles. Each child is treated as an individual and not forced into a particular mold, with the premise that children's learning ultimately takes place in self-chosen moments of intense concentration. The method was developed by Maria Montessori, an Italian educator who lived from 1870 to 1952.

MPA Abbreviation for the college degree *master of public administration*.

MS Abbreviation for the college degree *master of science*.

multiple-choice test A test in which several possible answers are given and the student has to choose among them rather than provide an individual response. A few years ago it was justifiable to criticize multiple-choice testing because it seemed reductive. Critics charged that the questions focused on memorized facts and did not encourage thinking. However, test designers took up the challenge to make more sophisticated multiple-choice tests. In many cases multiple-choice tests now require considerable thought, even notes and calculations, before choosing a bubble. (Sometimes called *controlled choice* or *selected response*.)

Muslim Students' Association The Muslim Students' Association, or Muslim Student Union, of the United States and Canada, also known as MSA National, is a religious organization dedicated to establishing and maintaining Islamic societies on college campuses in Canada and the United States. It serves to provide coordination and support for affiliated MSA chapters in colleges across North America. Established in 1963, the organization now has chapters in colleges across the continent, and is the precursor of the Islamic Society of North America and several other Islamic organizations.

NAEP The National Assessment of Educational Progress, also known as the *Nation's Report Card*. Students selected to take it form a statistically representative sample of the nation's students. Not all schools in a district and or even all students in the school will take the test. NAEP tests students in fourth, eighth, and 12th grade every two years in reading and mathematics and at longer intervals in other academic subjects such as science, history, and geography. NAEP is a criterion-referenced test. Its test items are derived from the NAEP Frameworks, the documents that act as national standards for NAEP. The tests combine multiple-choice, and short- and long-answer items. Results are reported in four levels: below basic, basic, proficient, and advanced. Separate scores are reported for groups of students based on characteristics such as race, ethnicity, family income, and gender. NAEP does not provide scores for individual students or schools.

National Merit Scholarship Corporation (NMSC) An independent, not-for-profit organization established in 1955 that operates without government assistance. NMSC conducts the National Merit Scholarship Program and the National Achievement Scholarship Program—annual competitions for recognition and college undergraduate scholarships.

NCES   The National Center for Education Statistics, the primary federal entity for collecting and analyzing data related to education.

New Century High Schools Initiative   A program designed to improve large, underperforming high schools by transforming them into small schools with links to community organizations. New Century High Schools each have about 400 students; the small size is intended to foster strong relationships between students and educators. These schools commit to a broad set of educational principles, but are free to make their own choices about curriculum.

New Chance   A program of the U.S. Department of Education for young welfare mothers who have dropped out of school that aims to improve both their employment potential and their parenting skills. Participants take GED (General Educational Development) preparation classes and complete a parenting and life skills curriculum. Once they complete this first phase of the program, they can receive occupational training and job placement assistance from New Chance, which also offers case management and child care.

No Child Left Behind   An act of Congress passed in January 2008, based upon the theories of standards-based education reform. The act requires states to develop their own standards and to test all students in certain grades in order to receive federal education funding. (Sometimes referred to as the NCLB, pronounced "nicklebee.").

normal school   An institute for the training of teachers.

norm-referenced test   A test that evaluates a student based upon where that student's score places him within a given population. (Often referred to as "NRT.") Norm-referenced assessment can be contrasted with criterion-referenced assessment and ipsative assessment. The curve-governed design of norm-referenced tests means that they do not compare the students' achievement to standards for what they should know and be able to do—they only compare students to other students who are assumed to be in the same norm group. The Educators' Handbook on Effective Testing (2002) lists the norms frequently used by major testing publishers. For example, the available norms for the Iowa Test of Basic Skills are: districts of similar sizes, regions of the country, socio-economic status, ethnicity, and type of school (e.g., public, Catholic, private non-Catholic) in addition to a representation of students nationally.

open-ended test A test that asks students to respond either by writing a few sentences in short answer form, or by writing an extended essay. Open-ended questions are also known as *constructed response* because test-takers must construct their response as opposed to selecting a correct answer. The advantage of open-ended items is that they allow a student to display knowledge and apply critical thinking skills. It is particularly difficult to assess writing ability, for example, without an essay or writing sample. The disadvantage is that constructed-response items require human readers, although attempts are being made to develop computer programs to score essays. Short-answer questions can be scored by looking for key terms since they often do not ask for complete sentences. But many state assessments ask for an extended essay, often in separate tests from the one used to report AYP.

outcomes-based education An education reform model that involves measuring individual student performance, statistics for which are called *outcomes*. This contrasts with traditional education, which primarily focuses on the resources that are available to the student, which are called *inputs*. Outcomes-based education was largely rejected in the United States as unworkable in the 1990s. (Often referred to as "OBE.")

paideia In ancient Greek, the word *paideia* means "education" or "instruction." Paideia was the process of educating humans into their true form, the real and genuine human nature. Since self-government was important to the Greeks, paideia, combined with ethos (habits), made a man good and made him capable as a citizen or a king. This education was not about learning a trade or an art but was about training for liberty (freedom) and nobility (the beautiful). Paideia is the cultural heritage that is continued through the generations. The Greeks considered paideia to be carried out by the aristocratic class, who were said to have intellectualized their culture and their ideas; the culture and the youth are then molded to the ideal.

parochial school A school that engages in religious education in addition to conventional education.

pedagogy The science and craft of education. From the Greek root that means "to lead the child."

PhD Abbreviation for the college degree *doctor of philosophy*, this degree entitles the recipient to the title "doctor." The PhD is the highest level of education that can be awarded in any field, and is usually required for those seeking a career as university professors.

PISA Program for International Student Assessment. Every three years tests 15-year-olds in industrialized countries on knowledge and skills essential for participation in 21th-century society. It is a matrix and criterion-referenced test that provides important information about the educational achievement of U.S. students compared to their peers worldwide.

Plessy v. Ferguson 1896 U.S. Supreme Court decision that made racial segregation legal.

portfolio A type of performance assessment that was popular before 2001, when state testing in accordance with NCLB came to dominate. Portfolios are collections of student work designed to show growth over a semester or a year. However, they are difficult to evaluate accurately, because their production and contents cannot be standardized. Both portfolios and performance assessment are now used as formative rather than summative assessment.

pre-kindergarten The first formal academic classroom-based learning environment that a child customarily attends in the United States before kindergarten. It begins around the age of four or five in order to prepare for the more didactic and academically intensive kindergarten. Pre-kindergarten was also known as "nursery school," but the term was phased out during the 1990s. (Also called "Pre-K" or "PK.")

preparatory school A secondary school, usually private, designed to prepare students for a college or university education. Some schools will also include a junior, or elementary, school. (Also known as "college prep school," or "prep school.")

preschool Education for children before the commencement of statutory education, usually between the ages of three and five. Preschool is also known as "nursery school," "day care," "pre-k," or "kindergarten."

primary school An institution where children receive the first stage of compulsory education known as primary or elementary education. Usually grades one through six.

▼

Private School Survey (PSS)   Conducted by the NCES, the PSS consists of a single survey that is completed by administrative personnel in private schools. Information collected includes: religious orientation, level of school, size of school, length of school year, length of school day, total enrollment (K-12), number of high school graduates, whether a school is single-sexed or coeducational and enrollment by sex, number of teachers employed, program emphasis, and existence and type of kindergarten program.

project-based learning   The use of classroom projects to drive the learning process, which in turn can be used to assess student's learning. It is also referred to as or PBL (or PjBL to avoid confusion with problem-based learning).

PSAT/NMSQT   The Preliminary SAT/National Merit Scholarship Qualifying Test, a program cosponsored by the College Board and National Merit Scholarship Corporation (NMSC). It is a standardized test that provides firsthand practice for the SAT. It also gives students a chance to enter NMSC scholarship programs and gain access to college and career planning tools. The PSAT/NMSQT measures critical reading skills, math problem-solving skills, and writing skills.

quadrivium   Arithmetic, astronomy, music, and geometry, four of the seven liberal arts set down by the Roman scholar Martianus Capella. The *quadrivium* was useful not just for keeping accounts, but an integral part of religion. Astronomy helped to determine the date and time, useful for keeping holidays, music was part of divine service, and geometry could be applied to measure land or build churches.

Quantum Opportunity Program (QOP)   An intensive and comprehensive program of the U.S. Department of Education for high school-aged youth that offers case management, mentoring, tutoring, and other education and support services. The program also offers financial incentives for participation in program activities. Participants enter QOP in the ninth grade and can receive services for four to five years, even if they drop out of school or move to another district.

reform mathematics   Mathematics standards for K–12 that give a strong call for a de-emphasis on manual arithmetic in favor of students' discovering their own knowledge and conceptual thinking. Reform mathematics curricula challenge students to make sense of new mathematical ideas through explorations and projects, often in real contexts. Reform texts emphasize written and verbal communication, working in cooperative groups, making connections between concepts, and connections between representations. By contrast, "traditional" textbooks emphasize procedural mathematics and provide step-by-step examples with skill exercises. Reform mathematics is one name for mathematics instruction based on recommendations originally published in 1989 by the National Council of Teachers of Mathematics (NCTM).

rubrick   A guide to scoring that provides a detailed description of essays that should be given a particular score (frequently one to six points, with six being the best). After extensive training with models of each score, two readers rate an essay independently. If their scores differ, a third reader reads the essay without knowing the two preceding scores. Group scoring of essays has a long history and has proved to be remarkably reliable.

SAT   A privately owned national test that many colleges and universities require as part of a student's application package. For most of its history the SAT, which is owned by the College Board but designed and administered by the Educational Testing Service, was deliberately not connected to any state or school's curriculum. Because it was designed to predict college success, at least as far as the freshman year, many regarded it as an aptitude rather than achievement test. However, the SAT recently underwent a major and widely publicized redesign to "better reflect what students study in high school." One of the changes is that the formerly all multiple-choice test now includes a writing sample, an essay scored by readers.

scale score   A numeric score that shows the overall performance on a standardized test. Usually a raw score (number of questions answered correctly) is converted to a scale score according to the difficulty of the test. (For example, the 200–800 scale used for the SAT.)

school district   The primary administrative unit for most public school systems. School districts are usually composed of an elected school board and a superintendent who acts as an executive of sorts. They are unique structures in American democracy, usually distinct from town, city, or state governance, but vested with similar powers of taxation and eminent domain. In cases of serious student or employee misconduct, the school district can also act as a sort of judicial system—for instance, imposing fines or terminating an employee.

secondary education   Secondary education is the stage of education following primary school. Secondary education is generally the final stage of compulsory education. The next stage of education is usually college or university.

Socratic method   A form of inquiry and debate between individuals with opposing viewpoints based on asking and answering questions to stimulate rational thinking and to illuminate ideas. It is a dialectical method, often involving an oppositional discussion in which the defense of one point of view is pitted against the defense of another; one participant may lead another to contradict himself in some way, strengthening the inquirer's own point. It is named after the Classical Greek philosopher Socrates.

Sophists   A class of itinerant intellectuals in fifth century B.C.E. Greece who taught courses in "excellence" or "virtue," speculated about the nature of language and culture, and employed rhetoric to achieve their purposes, generally to persuade or convince others. Sophists claimed that they could find the answers to all questions. Most of these sophists are known today primarily through the writings of their opponents (specifically Plato and Aristotle). Their attacks against Socrates (in fictional prosecution speeches) prompted a vigorous condemnation from his followers, including Plato and Xenophon, as there was a popular view of Socrates as a sophist. Their attitude, coupled with the wealth garnered by many of the sophists, eventually led to popular resentment against sophist practitioners and the ideas and writings associated with sophism.

standardized test   A test designed in such a way that the questions, conditions for administering, scoring procedures, and interpretations are consistent and administered and scored in a predetermined, standard manner. Students take the same test in the same conditions at the same time, if possible, so results can be attributed to student performance and not to differences in the administration or form of the test. For this reason, the results of standardized tests can be compared across schools, districts, or states. Standardized testing is sometimes used as a shorthand expression for machine scored multiple-choice tests; however, standardized tests can have almost any format.

standards-based education   Educational theory popular in the United States since 1980, which emphasizes setting objective standards by which to assess student progress, as opposed to norm-referenced ranking, which ranks a student relative to a given population of students.

status model   A method for measuring how students perform at one point in time; for example, the percent of fourth graders scoring at proficient or above in 2006.

summative assessment   Summative assessment records the state of student learning at certain end points in a student's academic career—at the end of a school year, or at certain grades such as grades 3, 5, 8, and 11. It literally "sums up" what students have learned. Summative assessment provokes most of the controversy about testing because it includes "high-stakes, standardized" testing carried out by the states.

talent development high schools   A school reform model for restructuring large high schools with persistent attendance and discipline problems, poor student achievement, and high dropout rates. The model includes both structural and curriculum reforms. It calls for schools to reorganize into small "learning communities"—including ninth-grade academies for first-year students and career academies for students in upper grades—to reduce student isolation and anonymity. It also emphasizes high academic standards and provides all students with a college-preparatory academic sequence.

Talent Search   A program of the U.S. Department of Education to help low-income and first-generation college students (those whose parents do not have four-year college degrees) complete high school and gain access to college through a combination of services designed to improve academic achievement and increase access to financial aid. Services include test taking and study skills assistance, academic advising, tutoring, career development, college campus visits, and financial aid application assistance.

technical college   A school that provides post-secondary training in technical and mechanical fields, focusing on vocational skills primarily at a community college level—parallel and sometimes equivalent to the first two years at a bachelor's-granting institution. (Also known as a *technical institute*.)

tenure   A tenured professor has a lifetime appointment until retirement, except for dismissal with "due cause." The reason

Fast
Facts

The New Face of Vocational Schools

With the changing economy and job-free recession recovery, vocational schools are no longer seen as "second-best" choices for those not suited to a two- or four-year school. Anecdotal evidence indicates that many vocational schools are welcoming those with associate's or even four-year degrees who want to make themselves more marketable in a highly competitive employment market—or at least wait out unfavorable conditions. Second-career changers are also finding their way to vocational schools, especially with many government incentives offering money to those who go back to retool their skills. Others are older workers looking to make their way in a data-centric world. "I'm tired of getting laid off at factories. I need to re-educate myself," said Patricia Parker, a 58-year-old business system technology student from Centerville, Tennessee, in a 2009 *USA Today* article. "I'm getting older. This factory work is killing me."

for the existence of such a privileged position is the principle of academic freedom, which holds that it is beneficial for state, society, and academy in the long run if learned persons are free to examine, hold, and advance controversial views without fear of losing their jobs. Tenure allows professors to engage in current political or other controversies. The argument has also been made that tenure actually diminishes academic freedom, as it forces all those seeking tenured positions to profess to the same views (political and academic) as those deciding who is awarded a tenured position. While it is true that after receiving tenure, the academic is free to pursue other theories, the degree of preparation and specialization required before being able to make a meaningful contribution to such theories and the lengthy period of time before tenure is granted means that the academic will be severely handicapped in contributing to any parts of their field other than the dominant paradigm. This is even more so now that many academics are being forced to spend several years in non-tenure track positions before beginning the five to six year process of gaining tenure. In certain jurisdictions, tenure is also granted to schoolteachers at primary and secondary schools, following a probationary period.

tenure-track   A teaching position for which the teacher or professor may eventually be granted tenure.

TIMSS   Trends in International Mathematics and Science Study. An international test that reports on science and mathematics achievement at grades four and eight. It is a matrix and criterion-referenced test that provides important information about the educational achievement of U.S. students compared to their peers worldwide.

Title IX   Title IX of the Education Amendments of 1972, also known as the Patsy T. Mink Equal Opportunity in Education Act, but more commonly known simply as Title IX. It is a U.S. law that states: "No person in the United States shall, on the basis of sex, be excluded from participation in, be denied the benefits of, or be subjected to discrimination under any education program or activity receiving Federal financial assistance." Although the most prominent "public face" of Title IX is its impact on high school and collegiate athletics, the original statute made no reference to athletics.

trivium   Grammar, logic, and rhetoric, three of the seven liberal arts set down by the Roman scholar Martianus Capella. The *trivium* allowed one to read and write in Latin, which would remain the language of the educated until modern times, as well as to share one's ideas and speak publicly—the main means of communication before print.

Twelve Together   A one-year peer support and mentoring program of the U.S. Department of Education for middle and early high school students that offers weekly after-school discussion groups led by trained volunteer adult facilitators. Each peer discussion group consists of about 12 participants, who are a mix of students at high risk of academic failure and others at lower academic risk. Group discussions are based on student interest, usually focusing on personal, family, and social issues. The program also offers homework assistance, trips to college campuses, and an annual weekend retreat.

umbrella school   An alternative education school that serves to oversee the homeschooling of children to fulfill government educational requirements. Some umbrella schools offer group classes, a defined curriculum, sports, field trips, standardized testing, and more. Others exist only to collect the minimal legal requirements. Some follow a specific faith, while others are secular.

university An institution of higher education and research that grants academic degrees and provides both undergraduate education and postgraduate education.

value-added model A method of measuring the degree in which teachers, schools, or education programs improve student performance.

vertical scale scores Numeric scores on standardized tests constructed so that the scale used for scoring is the same for two or more grade levels. Hence, a student's scale score gain over multiple years represents the student's level of academic growth over that period of time.

virtual education Instruction in a learning environment where teacher and student are separated by time or space, or both. Students receive course content and communicate with the teacher via course management applications, multimedia resources, the Internet, videoconferencing, and so on. (Also known as *distance learning.*)

vocational school A school in which students are taught the skills needed to perform a particular job. Traditionally, vocational schools have not existed to further education in the sense of liberal arts, but rather to teach only job-specific skills, and can be considered to be institutions devoted to training, not education. That purely vocational focus began changing in the 1990s toward broader academic and technical skills of students, as well as the vocational.

What Works Clearinghouse (WWC) Established in 2002 by the U.S. Department of Education's Institute of Education Sciences to provide educators, policymakers, and the public with a central and trusted source of scientific evidence of what works in education. The WWC is administered by the Department, through a contract to a joint venture of the American Institutes for Research and the Campbell Collaboration. To provide information needed by decision-makers, the WWC reviews and reports on existing studies of interventions (education programs, products, practices, and policies) in selected topic areas. WWC reviews of the evidence apply a set of standards that follow scientifically valid criteria for determining the effectiveness of these interventions.

whole language   A literacy philosophy that emphasizes that children should focus on meaning and strategy instruction. Language is treated as a complete meaning-making system, the parts of which function in relational ways. It is often contrasted with phonics-based methods of teaching reading and writing, which emphasize instruction for decoding and spelling. The whole language approach has drawn criticism by those who advocate "back to basics" pedagogy.

yeshivah   Generally a Jewish day school providing secular and religious instruction, but the term also applies to orthodox Jewish rabbinical seminaries.

Chapter 6

Resources

This chapter provides resources for both the "need to know" and the "nice to know." There are listings for job sources, ongoing training, associations, and unions. Periodicals to help you stay current with what is going on in education, including technology, are also listed. Some of the sources here offer practical information in the classroom, and others give a glimpse into the more administrative side. Several of the associations and organizations listed below function as labor unions, offer educational seminars, and provide networking opportunities.

Associations and Organizations

Associations and organizations are vital for education professionals. Besides offering opportunities to exchange ideas, theories, and cutting-edge pedagogical practices, they can be places to help continue one's own education, as well.

American Association of Colleges for Teacher Education (AACTE) is a national alliance of educator preparation programs dedicated to professional development of teachers and PK-12 school leaders. The 800 institutions holding AACTE membership represent public and private colleges and universities in every state, the District of Columbia, the Virgin Islands, Puerto Rico, and Guam. AACTE's reach and influence fuel its mission of serving learners by providing all school personnel with superior training and continuing education. (http://www.aacte.org)

American Board for Certification of Teacher Excellence (ABCTE) is an organization for people who already have a bachelor's degree and are changing careers. They offer certification programs in many different subject areas. A note of warning, however: their certification training does not seem to be accepted by many states (it can be used for some programs in Florida, Idaho, and a few other states). (http://www.abcte.org)

American Federation of Teachers (AFT) publishes a number of journals and newspapers, including *American Teacher*, their

Everyone
Knows

The Ivy League

"Ivy League" is virtually synonymous with elite higher education and tradition, to such a degree that it is almost impossible for anyone to imagine a way to reach any higher. Parents the world over insist that their children will attend an "ivy league" school. However, the Ivies are not the oldest schools in the United States: While seven of the nine oldest colleges in the United States are in the Ivy League (Harvard, Yale, the University of Pennsylvania, Princeton, Columbia, and Dartmouth), Rutgers and William and Mary were also founded in the colonial era. (The eighth Ivy, Cornell, was founded in 1865.) Likewise, many of the top-ranked undergraduate institutions are not in the Ivy League. For instance, Amherst and Williams colleges, both located in Massachusetts, continually vie for the number one ranking.

The Ivy League actually originated as a sports league, with a series of written and unwritten understandings between the various schools, which shared a common culture and reputation for elitism. It became official after the NCAA Division I was founded in 1954. The name came from *New York Tribune* sportswriter Caswell Adams, who in 1933 made a disparaging remark concerning Harvard and Princeton's football teams, saying that New York's Fordham University would easily trounce them as "they're only ivy league." The name stuck.

monthly newspaper, and *American Educator*, their quarterly magazine. They also have a special section on starting a career as a
teacher. (http://www.aft.org)

The Learning Annex is a non-traditional teaching workshop business. They sponsor courses covering everything from wine tast-
ing to book binding to how to shoot your own video—anything
they think people will pay money to learn. It is not easy to make a
living at this type of education. Most people who make money at
it do it to advertise a business they have elsewhere. But some people make the bulk of their income from going around the country
teaching these types of seminars. The key is that the tuition fee is
not where the money is; the money is in back of the room sales.
People will pay to hear a lecture, buy a book that is basically a
transcript of that lecture, buy a video of the same lecture, attend
a "webinar" which is a repeat of that lecture, and then pay extra
to attend an "extended version" of the lecture where they will
get more personal attention over a longer period of time, usually
two days. This is what Robert Alan in his book *Multiple Streams
of Income* calls "the money funnel." There are not many places to
go for information on this corner of the education industry. One
place is the Learning Annex itself, if there is a branch near you.
They actually hold classes on how to teach seminars at the learning annex. Of course, what they want you to do is sign up for
their two day extended version of the class, where they will help
you design the curriculum and prepare materials, but that is the
way these things operate. (http://www.learningannex.com)

National Board for Professional Teaching Standards (NBPTS)
was established to create a set of national certification standards.
The idea was to eventually create "board certification" for teachers
similar to the systems in place for doctors, lawyers, accountants,
and engineers. NBPTS certifies teachers in a number of different
subject areas, and some states accept NBPTS certification as the
certification program of teacher training. If you are looking to
get certification in a particular subject, be it art, history, science,
or others (they have 27 certificate areas) NBPTS is a great place
to go. Because their standards are rigorous, NBPTS certification
looks great on your CV. (http://www.nbpts.org)

**National Council for Accreditation of Teacher Education
(NCATE)** is the profession's mechanism to help establish high
quality teacher preparation. Through the process of professional
accreditation of schools, colleges, and departments of education,

NCATE works to make a difference in the quality of teaching and teacher preparation. NCATE's performance-based system of accreditation fosters competent classroom teachers and other educators who work to improve the education of all K–12 students. (http://www.ncate.org)

National Education Association (NEA) is the largest labor union in the Untied States and represents teachers, administrators, college faculty, and even college students preparing to become teachers. Most of their resources are geared toward current teachers, but there are a number of useful resources for new teachers. However, most of these are in the "members only" section. (http://www.nea.org)

National School Boards Association (NSBA) supports school boards nationwide with advocacy, legislation, school governance, policies, health, law, and training. (http://www.nsba.org)

Skill Path is a business-training provider that runs corporate seminars and retreats. Associated with Graceland University, they teach more than 20,000 "how-to" sessions to over 500,000 people in 450 cities. There arc numerous other seminar and retreat providers. (http://www.skillpath.com)

Books and Periodicals

Use the following books to both inspire and advise you as you begin to carve a niche for yourself in the field of education. Even if you have some teaching experience, these selections will still prove useful as you continue to hone your craft.

Books

Because We Can Change the World: A Practical Guide To Building Cooperative, Inclusive Classroom Communities. By Mara Sapon-Shevin (Allyn & Bacon, 1998). With the increase of diverse students in all classrooms, pre-service and in-service teachers often find themselves overwhelmed with how to provide a quality learning community that is inclusive of all students. This book delivers hope, promise, and practical goals for teachers who wish to create a warm, respectful, and nurturing learning environment for their students that will, in turn, inspire students to make a difference in their classroom community and the world beyond. Discussing theory through vignettes and presenting practical activities, the book helps teachers show children how to understand and accept differences among themselves and in the world in a way that empowers them to make a difference.

A Conception of Teaching. By Nathaniel Gage (Springer, 2008). A classic work on the theory and philosophy of teaching. Gage combines cognitive theory and pedagogy and filters this through years of research as a professor of education. It is an influential and important work on how students learn.

The Courage to Teach: Exploring the Inner Landscape of a Teacher's Life. By Parker Palmer (Jossey-Bass, 1997). As a spiritually inspirational book for teachers, *The Courage to Teach* is one of the best. The premise is concise and unarguable: good teaching comes from the identity and the integrity of the teacher. Teachers are encouraged to turn their inquiring minds inward—developing a deeper understanding of what it means to fulfill the spiritual calling of teaching. Good teachers share one trait, says author Parker Palmer: they are able to weave a complex web of connections among themselves, their subjects, and their students, so that students can learn to weave a world for themselves.

Escalante: The Best Teacher in America. By Jay Matthews (Henry Holt, 1988). One of several books on Jaime Escalante, the East Los Angeles math teacher who was the subject of the movie *Stand and Deliver.* Escalante is something of an icon of teaching: an immigrant from Latin America who had trouble even finding work as a teacher when he arrived in this country, who became famous for challenging his inner city students to take difficult math and physics classes. In spite of resistance from faculty and administration, he got his students to excel in mathematics.

A Hope in the Unseen: An American Odyssey from the Inner City to the Ivy League. By Ron Suskind (Broadway, 1999). The author won the Pulitzer Prize for feature writing in 1995 for his stories on Cedric Jennings, a talented black teenager struggling to succeed in one of the worst public high schools in Washington, D.C. Suskind expanded those features into a full-length nonfiction narrative, following Jennings beyond his high-school graduation to Brown University, and in the tradition of Leon Dash's *Rosa Lee* and Alex Kotlowitz's *There Are No Children Here*, delivers a compelling story on the struggles of inner-city life in modern America.

The Kindness of Children. By Vivian Gussin Paley (Harvard University Press, 2000). A former kindergarten teacher, a MacArthur Award recipient, and the prolific author of many books about children and

Best
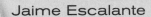
Practice

Jaime Escalante

By now, the story of Jaime Escalante's inspiring, prodding, and pushing inner-city high school students to pass the AP Calculus exam is well-known. What is lesser known is the aftermath.

At the height of Garfield High's program, in 1987, 85 students passed the AP Calculus exams. The following year, the movie and book were released, and Escalante found himself a celebrity. However, the movie made it seem as if failing students could be transformed into achievers overnight. None of this would have been possible, however, without the support of Garfield principal Henry Gradillas, who established a "pipeline" to get Garfield students ready to take the calculus class. When Gradillas went on sabbatical to complete his doctorate in 1988, he was not brought back to Garfield. Escalante had had to set a number of workplace rules by the wayside, such as the limit on class sizes.

However, the new administration was not as tolerant of Escalante's bucking union and school rules to achieve his ends as Gradillas had been, and before long, both he and his co-teachers left. In order to build his pioneering calculus program, Escalante had had to violate professional guidelines. This may have been technically against the rules, but highlights an important fact in today's legalistic teaching profession: Often, the only way out of stifling bureaucracy is if teachers and administrators cooperate.

education, describes how very young students transform themselves and one another by taking in, narrating, and sometimes dramatically acting out tales of kindness and other acts of goodness. Beginning with the true account of Teddy, a multi-handicapped boy in a London school who wears a padded helmet and is treated sensitively by a normal student, she delves into the matter of how children, at their best, find ways of reaching out to those in need, thus allowing themselves and their peers to grow morally.

Other People's Children: Cultural Conflict in the Classroom. By Lisa Delpit (New Press, 2006). MacArthur fellow and educator Delpit argues that many minority students are erroneously labeled "underachievers" due to failures of communication between teachers and students.

Periodicals

Every magazine has an online presence nowadays. Nearly all of these have meaningful content available at the site listed, but some of them require subscriptions to access portions of the site.

The Chronicle of Higher Education is published every weekday. It features news, advice, and jobs for people in academe. The Chronicle's Web site posts the complete contents of the latest issue, as well as daily news and advice columns, current job listings, articles published since September 1989, discussion forums, and career-building tools. (http://chronicle.com)

Converge Magazine has a wide range of content and interactive links, including editorials, events, awards, literacy, papers, blogs, grants and recordings. (http://www.convergemag.com)

Early Childhood News contains articles about child development, developmentally appropriate practices, health and safety, behavior and guidance, and assessment. It also highlights ideas for teaching infants, toddlers, preschoolers and school-age children; ideas for activities and craft projects; and links to the offices that regulate licensed child care in each of the 50 states. (http://www.earlychildhoodnews.com)

Education Week covers local, state, and national news and issues from preschool through the 12th grade. Published by the non-profit Editorial Projects in Education Inc., which also publishes the *Teacher Professional Development Sourcebook, Digital Directions,* Edweek.org, Teachermagazine.org, and TopSchoolJobs.org. (http://www.edweek.org)

ESL Magazine is for teachers of American English and ESL/EFL professionals, with the news, trends, methods, products and services that matter to them. (http://www.eslmag.com)

From Now On is an education technology journal. E-mail subscription is free. (http://www.fno.org)

Scholastic publishes several magazines. Those for teachers include *Instructor Magazine, Early Childhood Today,* and *School Jobs Now;* those for kids include *Clifford the Big Red Dog, Let's Find Out, Math, Science World, Choices, Art,* and *The New York Times Upfront.* The site also includes teaching resources, student activities, a "book wizard," class homepage builder, book clubs, classroom magazines, and links to the Scholastic magazines. (http://www.scholastic.com)

Other Media: Films

Although none here are strictly documentaries, these tremendously inspiring films provide a dramatic, yet balanced perspective on the teaching profession.

The Blackboard Jungle (1955) Inner-city high school teacher Richard Dadier struggles to maintain his idealism in this gritty drama set in the 1950s. The students drink, smoke, steal and cause mayhem, and two of Dadier's delinquents duke it out to be crowned leader of their classroom turf. This film was the first major motion picture with a rock 'n' roll soundtrack, which includes "Rock Around the Clock."

Dangerous Minds (1995) In this blackboard-jungle drama, Louanne Johnson, an erstwhile lady leatherneck turned teacher squares off against a classroom of impudent, inner-city teens. The students' bullying tactics nearly drive Johnson out the first day, but she radically changes her lesson plan to include bribery and browbeating (despite objections from the principal) in an effort to teach the class that learning is its own reward.

Dead Poets Society (1989) John Keating is an unconventional English teacher who lives by a simple motto: Seize the day! Neil Perry is a prep school student who dreams of being an actor but lives in fear of his imperious father, who wants to see him matriculated into Harvard's medical school. The screenplay won an Oscar.

Goodbye Mr. Chips (1939, 1969) Latin instructor Mr. Chipping comes to teach at Brookfield private boys' school in the 1870s. Now an old-timer in the 1920s, "Mr. Chips" thinks back on his career, his various friends, co-workers and pupils.

Mr. Holland's Opus (1995) In 1965, passionate musician Glenn Holland takes a day job as a high school music teacher, convinced it is just a small obstacle on the road to his true calling: writing a historic opus. As the decades roll by with the composition unwritten but generations of students inspired through his teaching, Holland must redefine his life's purpose.

October Sky (1999) As the Soviet satellite Sputnik streaks across the heavens in October 1957, it is a source of inspiration for 17-year-old Homer Hickam, who refuses to follow in his father's footsteps laboring in West Virginia's coal mines. Homer would rather reach for the stars—literally. Drafting a few friends, he sets about crafting a rocket to compete for a science-fair scholarship—and a chance to change his seemingly immutable future.

Stand and Deliver (1987) A moving, mostly-true story of famed East L.A. math teacher Jaime Escalante, who finds himself in a classroom of rebellious remedial-math students. He stuns fellow faculty members with his plans to teach AP Calculus, and even more when the mostly Hispanic teens overcome the odds and eventually go the distance.

Teachers (1984) Threatened by the bad publicity of a class action lawsuit, the administration at JFK High School is looking to weed out any teachers who are critical of the school's policies, most notably student favorite Alex Jurel. Fighting to save his job, Jurel disregards the school board's wishes and continues his mission to help the "problem" students whom the school seems all too willing to ignore.

To Sir With Love (1967) Sidney Poitier stars as Mark Thackeray, an engineer by training who reluctantly takes a teaching job in a working-class London high school. His unruly students assume they will easily gain the upper hand. Poitier, of course, has other ideas. Eventually he wins the students over, changing their lives—and his—in the process.

Up the Down Staircase (1967) Sylvia Barrett, a green but idealistic young teacher takes a job at a tough inner-city high school. Troubled by the apathy of her students and fellow teachers, Barrett revels in her few successes. But her naïveté may prove a fatal flaw, despite her good intentions. (An adaptation of Bel Kaufman's novel.)

Web Sites

Peruse the Web sites below to find information about professional requirements, educational institutions, job postings, and innumerable other pieces of valuable career advice.

All Education Schools is perhaps the best, or at least the most detailed "how to" site, designed as a jumping off point for people who are considering a career in teaching. Here you will find information on teaching colleges (both online and brick-and-

Keeping in Touch

Friends and Mentors

Remember that just as you want to have an effect on your students' lives, so too do your old professors and teachers want to know how *you* are doing. Be sure to drop a line to those who have influenced you in some way. Not only will it make their day, but they will be gratified to hear how you are passing on their legacy. (Plus—who knows?—they might have some helpful career advice or know of an open position!)

mortar), articles on how to become a teacher and why anyone would want to, and breakdowns of teaching careers by specialty. There breakdowns by state are extremely useful. (http://www.alleducationschools.com)

Certification Map is a great site at which to find out the credential requirements for each state. It lists education and teaching requirements, average salaries, and how to get credentialed. It also has some other useful stats. Want to teach in Iowa? You will need prerequisite coursework in your field and do fieldwork to get certified. However, they have reciprocity with forty different states. Rather teach in New York? Good choice: the average teacher's salary is about $64,000. That is good, but this is great: it is 133 percent of the average salary of all professions in the state. (http://certificationmap.com)

Department of Education is an exceptionally comprehensive government site. In addition to press releases and announcements from the Department of Education, you will also find a great number of resources for current and aspiring teachers. The most important of these is probably financial aid. The Department of Education handles nearly all financial aid programs for the federal government, including both grants and loans. The number and variety of grants available may surprise you and, in fact, there are grants specifically for those who want to become teachers. For instance TEACH, which stands for Teacher Education Assistance for College and Higher education provides up to $4,000 a year for persons who intend to become elementary or secondary school teachers serving low income families. They also maintain links to several other useful websites for aspiring teachers. (http://www.ed.gov)

Education.org is a clearinghouse for online education. They also have some good reference articles on how to become a teacher with useful links at http://www.education.org/articles/teacher-certification-and-continuing-education.html. (http://www.education.org)

Education Resources Information Center (ERIC) is an online digital library of education research and information sponsored by the Institute of Education Sciences (IES) of the U.S. Department of Education. ERIC provides ready access to education literature to support the use of educational research and information to improve practice in learning, teaching, educational decision-making, and research. The online face of ERIC is a comprehensive, easy-to-use, searchable, Internet-based bibliographic and full-text database of education research and information that also meets the requirements of the Education Sciences Reform Act of 2002. (http://www.eric.ed.gov)

Education World is an omnibus site with resources on lesson planning, professional development, administration, technology integration, and many links. (http://www.educationworld.com)

ENC is a subscription service that offers math and science resources from professional development to lesson plans. (http://www.goenc.com)

Job Banks for Teachers are similar to national job hunting sites like Monster and Hotjobs, but focus on teaching positions. Use the following to locate available positions: *ABC Teaching Jobs* (http://www.abcteachingjobs.com); *Education America* (http://www.educationamerica.org); *Teacher Jobs* (http://www.teacherjobs.com); and *Teaching Jobs* (http://www.teachers-teachers.com).

So You Wanna has a lot of helpful information and links. You will find advice on starting your career, picking a specialization, and finding a college where you can do teacher training, and a few warnings as to the pitfalls and trials of a life in education. (http://www.soyouwanna.com/site/syws/teacher/teacher3.html)

Teachers-Teachers is a national job listing affiliated with the NEA. They post teaching jobs in every state and territory. Membership is free. (http://www.teachers-teachers.com)

Teacher Vision is one of the best sites on the Internet for current teachers. This is a one-stop resource for teaching materials and pedagogy. Focusing on K–12 classroom instruction, they have lesson plans, subject guides, handouts, visual aids, and tips on classroom organization. It is extremely useful as a place for new teachers to get ideas about how to go about their jobs. (http://www.teachervision.fen.com)

Teach for America is a program where recent college graduates in any field teach for two years in low-income communities. One really interesting article on the website is on alternative routes to teacher certification (http://www.ed.gov/admins/tchrqual/recruit/altroutes/index.html). This is mostly a guide to setting up such programs, but it includes a number of examples that could be useful for people who wish to jump into teaching without having to go through certification right away. (http://www.teachforamerica.org)

Teach-Nology is an online teacher resources with links to rubrics, games, teaching tips, lesson plans and periodicals. (http://www.teach-nology.com)

Troops to Teachers is a program run by the Department of Defense that seeks to move recently discharged troops into primary education jobs. (http://www.ed.gov/programs/troops/index.html)

Online Universities that Offer Teacher Education Programs

Ashford University offers bachelor of arts programs in early childhood education, arts in education and public policy, and early childhood education administration. (http://www.ashford.edu)

Kaplan offers several MS and MA programs in education. (http://www.kaplan.edu)

University of Phoenix is an online leader in continuing education. It has numerous degree programs in education. (http://www.phoenix.edu)

Western Governor's University was founded by the members of the non-partisan Western Governors Association in 1996. Today WGU is a non-profit fully accredited online university designed specifically to meet the educational needs of working adults. One of the areas WGU has always focused on is teacher preparation. They offer 18 online licensure programs for teachers, and are the only online university accredited by the National Council for the

Accreditation of Teacher Education. Teaching is done online with testing at testing centers. Not only that, but students can receive credit for knowledge they already have by testing out of subjects. One computer professional with 15 years of job experience received a bachelor's degree in two years by testing out of many of many of the required courses. WGU is already one of the top suppliers of math and science teachers to inner cities. Because it is not-for-profit (unlike other online universities), it is extremely affordable. Tuition is about $6,000 a year, which is less than most state-funded public universities. (http://www.wgu.edu)

Index